Routledge Revivals

The Poetry of Alexander Pope

First published in 1955, this exegesis on the writings of Alexander Pope reveals the technical felicities of his poetry, and is the first to be devoted to the great meaning inherent in his work. One section, which has appeared before and did much to redirect the study of Pope, has been thoroughly revised. Of the other four chapters, one offers an original of The Temple of Fame, and, while discussing this neglected poem, makes several suggestions which may be said to constitute a significant advance in aesthetics. Another analyses Byron's support of Pope, regarding it as a landmark in the history of English literary criticism and as necessary to the understanding of Pope and Byron alike. The last chapter discusses the relation of Pope's thought to our own time. This book adds much to what is already known of Pope, and will go far in reviving an interest in the work and philosophy of the Laureate of Peace.

I0884164

The Poetry of Alexander Pope

Laureate of Peace

George Wilson Knight

Routledge Revivals
Routledge
Taylor & Francis Group

First published in 1955
by Routledge & Kegan Paul

This edition first published in 2018 by Routledge
2 Park Square, Milton Park, Abingdon, Oxon, OX14 4RN
and by Routledge
711 Third Avenue, New York, NY 10017

Routledge is an imprint of the Taylor & Francis Group, an informa business

© 1955 George Wilson Knight

All rights reserved. No part of this book may be reprinted or reproduced or utilised in any form or by any electronic, mechanical, or other means, now known or hereafter invented, including photocopying and recording, or in any information storage or retrieval system, without permission in writing from the publishers.

Publisher's Note
The publisher has gone to great lengths to ensure the quality of this reprint but points out that some imperfections in the original copies may be apparent.

Disclaimer
The publisher has made every effort to trace copyright holders and welcomes correspondence from those they have been unable to contact.
A Library of Congress record exists under ISBN: 65029516

ISBN 13: 978-1-138-30713-1 (hbk)
ISBN 13: 978-1-315-14237-1 (ebk)
ISBN 13: 978-1-138-30749-0 (pbk)

The Poetry of Pope

LAUREATE OF PEACE

by

G. WILSON KNIGHT

Routledge and Kegan Paul
LONDON

First published in 1955
Published as a Routledge paperback 1965
by Routledge & Kegan Paul Ltd
Broadway House, 68–74 Carter Lane
London, E.C.4

© G. *Wilson Knight 1965*

No part of this book may be reproduced in any form without permission from the publisher, except for the quotation of brief passages in criticism

To

JOHN COWPER POWYS

artist, teacher, seer

in

admiration

Originally published as
LAUREATE OF PEACE: ON THE GENIUS OF ALEXANDER POPE

CONTENTS

PREFACE

On the presentation of this study—the first, so far as I know, to be devoted to the total contents, as opposed to the style in isolation, of Pope's poetic work—a few preliminary notes may prove helpful.

The book is composed of five sections, all but one of which are new. The opening is in the nature of a general survey intended to make a rough stage-setting for what follows.[1] This is followed by 'The Vital Flame', which appeared first in *The Burning Oracle* in 1939 and has been for long out of print. It has been given a surface revision, mainly a smoothing of syntax, and I have incorporated three or four new quotations, but nothing has been added to the thought. Since its first publication, this essay has helped to reorientate the contemporary understanding of Pope's poetry, particularly (as I note on pp. 48, 51 and 171–2 below with references to Professor Maynard Mack's important and standard edition[2]) in respect to the *Essay on Man*. Such defences are forced on me by the nature of the opposition which my methods of interpretative analysis are still, after twenty-five years, receiving in England. An attempt is made to clarify the issue in my third section, a study of the unjustly neglected *Temple of Fame*, in the course of which I have occasion to discuss the mutually interpretative functions of the arts of space and time in direct relation to my own technique of spatial interpretation.

The fourth section is given to Byron's praise of Pope. Of this I knew nothing when I composed 'The Vital Flame' some sixteen years ago, and, when I came across it during my Byronic studies, I was indeed gratified to find that my own understanding of Pope had been so closely paralleled by Byron. If I was mad in respecting

[1] I rather think that my characterizing (on pp. 7–9) of literary periods in terms of certain favoured mechanisms may owe something to a conversation with Professor Lewis Horrox some twenty years ago.

[2] I take this opportunity to pay my tribute to the excellence of the *Twickenham* edition, now nearing completion under the general editorship of John Butt.

Pope's 'message', in which he himself so ardently believed, I was mad in excellent company; and even those who most rigorously oppose my refusal to limit my studies to discussions of biography, sources, technique and the manipulation of language, will, I hope, agree that the triangle made of Pope's reiterated claims, Byron's ringing acceptations, and my own interpretations of both Pope and Byron is, to say the least, a self-consistent and harmonious entity. But to many readers it will, I hope, be rather more than that.

My final section discusses Pope's poetic thought in relation to our own time. It has for long been my practice, both as a university lecturer and as a writer, to insist at every turn that what we call great literature is only great to us in so far as it radiates living meanings, today; and it has always appeared to me both strange and sad that the treatment of literature as rooting backwards into sources and causes should in every age be academically honourable, while any attempt to establish contact with its forward pointings is considered the preserve only of amateurs and cranks. This contact can be greatly assisted by stage-production, or public reading: my own understanding of Pope was first awakened by listening to Professor D. Nichol Smith's reading of certain passages, during his lectures, at Oxford, in 1922.

Great poetry speaks to us with a living voice. When in the summer of 1950 my brother and I wanted words for a bronze tablet to be placed by a memorial tree to our mother in the Garden of Remembrance at Lawnswood, our choice fell on a couplet from the *Essay on Man*:

Safe in the hand of one disposing Pow'r,
Or in the natal, or the mortal hour.

That Pope should have provided the words we wanted is, perhaps, worth the recording; and it may also be worth recording that it seemed, to us at least, natural enough that such a need should be met by words of Pope.

It is a pleasant duty to acknowledge the courtesy of Messrs. John Lane the Bodley Head Ltd. and of Mr. John Cowper Powys in allowing me to use an extended quotation from Mr. Powys' *Rabelais*.

My line references to Pope and Shakespeare follow, respectively, the *Globe* and the *Oxford* texts.

G. W. K.

1954

I

DICTION AND DOCTRINE

I. DICTION AND DOCTRINE

At the start of the eighteenth century a new way of life was being established in England. The fruits of the Revolution were maturing. Under Queen Anne party politics were getting, if at first rather unsteadily, into their stride, as a safeguard against bloodier methods; new classes were rising rapidly to education, power, and prestige; there was peace and renewal after distraction and unrest. The age of Anne recaptured, in its own fashion, something of that assurance, and more than something of the harmony, of the age of Elizabeth I. Its poet was Pope: 'Be mine the blessings of a peaceful reign.'[1]

Dante, Shakespeare and Pope all reflect a unified and harmonious life-view; but Milton does not. The medieval synthesis assists Dante's creation of a circular system within which, like the figures on Keats' urn, the various turmoils of human existence could be placed. The problems handled by Shakespeare were, if not greater, certainly more involved. Dante used neither epic nor drama; neither physical nor spiritual conflict assumed even a provisional autonomy; all was settled, labelled, and in its place, and action at a discount. At a period of balance after civil turmoil and national victory, Shakespeare's work shows a subtle interplay of militaristic and spiritual conflict; the main emphasis falling on the spiritual, at most, except for *Henry V*, on civic or civil, conflict; and the expression is accordingly drama. There is not the controlling serenity of Dante, and yet, considering the great forces, medieval and Renaissance, at play, the resulting harmony is remarkable. The triumph is more a triumph of insight into the central stuff of man than a triumph for 'order' or 'tradition', though order and tradition are part of the final synthesis.[2]

[1] *Windsor Forest*, 366.

[2] For a discussion of the dangers to Shakespearian study of any too exclusive a

In Shakespeare the individual man's aspiring quest is variously contrasted with, overrules, or is subdued to, concepts and visions of harmony; tempests interweave with music, the music is wrenched out of, one with, the tempests; man himself becomes cosmic.

With Marlowe and Milton, in *Dr. Faustus*, in *Paradise Lost*, humanism is set against religion; the humanism is damned and yet damnation cannot silence its challenge. These works are great as symptoms of a dislocation, but their artistic integrity suffers: their technique is disrupted by the conflict it should resolve. The Elizabethan balance was, at the best, precarious. With the growing multiplication of divergent thought-streams and religious sects, together with the upstarting of dynastic nationalisms, in France pre-eminently, emphasis fell next on heroic action. Milton's great poem, half-epic, half-dramatic, feels the whole cosmos in self-conflict, and, as his iron technique clamps down on a hell of frustrated energies, the result is less harmony than torture; and the unresolved opposition of *Paradise Regained* does little to close the gap.

Cromwell's attempt at a theocracy overleaping the established ordinances of church and state led naturally to a military dictatorship; and that, by revulsion, forced a swerve back to the human; to the King; to the classical values. But, after the Restoration, the court, no less than Cromwell's dictatorship, reflected a part only of the nation. It remained parasitic, the organic relationships of the Shakespearian period being gone. In this hot-house atmosphere we find Dryden with consummate skill trying to make order from chaos.[1] Of innately Chaucerian affinities, he was, in general, a writer of clarity and common sense, and a firm supporter, though with little personal fire, of authority in state and church, leaving as his best record *Absalom and Achitophel*, with its satire on religious zeal and moral of submission to the throne. Dryden tends to put man in his place as firmly as any medievalist, while rating high, as the medievalist did not, the classic virtues, and hankering after heroism. At the Restoration drama had become pure, if sometimes rather impure, entertainment, without any such inward pressures and tensions as

concentration on the 'order' concept, see my 'Prefatory Note', with its 'Chart of Shakespeare's Dramatic Universe', to the 1953 re-issue of *The Shakespearian Tempest*.

[1] Dryden's poetry has been well handled in our time, pre-eminently by Mark van Doren's study (New York, 1920; London, 1931); by T. S. Eliot in his *Selected Essays* (1932); and by Bonamy Dobrée's *Restoration Tragedy* (1929).

you find in Shakespeare, Marlowe or Corneille; and this left Dryden free, without claiming more for man than his due, to *play* at heroics. He, or his audience, were half aware that the heroic ideal was a necessity, that the comprehensive system of Christendom was, in fact, dissolved, and that the Renaissance could not be written off as a blunder. The humanistic values of love and honour held compelling force over the mind, but it was less easy to place their resultant extravagances. Dryden's heroic plays record the attempt to give them a provisional placing in terms of entertainment.[1]

What Dryden lacked was a personal core to his life's work. It has, it is true, a key, in his search for order and authority, but those are mental concepts, and the core of a great poet's work cannot be merely conceptual; it will exist in the realm of symbolism, or reflect some great power of religion or nature; it will not be the product of human reason. Dryden does not attempt the extraordinary assimilations and harmonizations of Shakespeare; he does not plunge into the impossible task which Milton found beyond even his almost superhuman poetic strength; instead, he deploys his rich Chaucerian common sense over a mental world where religion is religion, science science, nature nature, man a creature of entertaining ambitions, and the king on his throne.

Pope's work, though profiting by the general tidying up that stands so firmly to Dryden's credit, has that pulsing heart for lack of which Dryden's remains a little cold; it is a single, organic, whole, as surely as Dante's or Shakespeare's; and it shows a wondrous harmony. How was that done?

First, we can say that it was done by selection. His concentration is focused on man, body and soul, felt in direct, even intimate, relation to nature, society, and the cosmos. With him the medieval is, if not exactly forgotten, certainly not stressed, nor is there any central reliance on Christian myth or dogma. Though himself a catholic by upbringing, his poetry is Christian in spirit rather than in form. His own satiric verse he sees as a 'sacred weapon', directed by 'Heaven', to be handled with reverence, inspired by a 'priestless muse', and opening 'eternity'.[2] Traditional religion is, it is true, nobly handled in

[1] And even, perhaps, *humour*. I am thinking of certain striking thoughts advanced by Douglas Jefferson in *The Significance of Dryden's Heroic Plays* in the Proceedings of the Leeds Philosophical Society, 1940, v, iii, 125–39, and *Aspects of Dryden's Imagery*, *Essays in Criticism*, Jan., 1954.

[2] *Satires, Epilogue*, II, 212–35.

the *Messiah* eclogue and *Eloisa to Abelard*, the last witnessing a profundity of religious feeling, but significantly deriving its extraordinary dramatic power from the opposition of natural impulse and transcendental authority. The *Essay on Man* builds its statement from a mass of pagan and Christian lore permeated throughout by the poet's own psychological and religious sensibilities, with as its heart and hinge a human doctrine of sublimation that forecasts the teaching of *Thus Spake Zarathustra*. We may say that his poetic universe flowers from a soil of classical-Renaissance humanism, though it is a matter rather of imaginative appeal than of learning or scholarship. Greece and Rome were guiding stars to him, and the heroic values are throughout emphatic. But there is no reliance on themes of war or social conflict; he is our only great poet since Shakespeare who has not left us a drama. His poetic universe is, moreover, peopled by delicate spirits and angelic hierarchies. More, it offers, as we shall see (pp. 46, 71–6, 179–80), a religious insight attuned to that of the Gospels and finally sharpened into a militant ethic recalling St. Paul; so that there is, as it were, *a New Testament structure about his life's work, as a whole* (p. 156 below). He is a poet of peace; his stage is mainly destitute of action, and epic themes, except for his translation of Homer, are only present through the medium of humour or burlesque. And yet, somehow, the heroic, the Renaissance, values are not only preserved, but emphatic; and in this successful marriage of New Testament and Renaissance lies the extraordinary importance of the accomplishment of his poetry and the secret of its unique composure.

Whether or not he can be called a 'deist' depends on our understanding of the term. If to write:

> *Safe in the hand of one disposing Pow'r,*
> *Or in the natal, or the mortal hour,*
>
> (*Essay on Man*, I, 287)

is to be a deist, the term can pass; otherwise, it cannot.[1] From the heterogeneous mass of philosophies and theologies that leave the seventeenth century an unweeded garden of riotous growth, he selects, prunes, and fertilizes. But it is a creative selection; he has felt the deep necessities, the real lines of force, and labours to give them

[1] I am thinking of the poetry. Writing from the more biographical standpoint, Bonamy Dobrée says: 'He was, in fact, as near as does not matter, a Deist' (*Alexander Pope*, 1951, II, 29).

encouragement and discipline. The vast field of speculation is narrowed down, as with heat-rays through a lens, to one burning spot. Therefore, though various philosophers, including St. Paul, may be contributory, he claims to be dominated by none;[1] he is neither in any *limited* sense Christian, nor is he anti-Christian; neither properly Whig nor Tory; he is as happy discussing philosophy with Bolingbroke as in visiting Cobham's patriots at Stowe. No labels apply, and yet his work is simple, lucid and coherent. In Pope, as in Shakespeare, what is best and most significant in his age, not in its thought merely, but in its life, becomes incandescent. But he is not, any more than Shakespeare, to be interpreted in the light of his—or any other—age; he is himself the light. He speaks for his age not only as a poet, but as a prophet; he makes his age, the little community of Augustan England, or London, prophetic; and prophetic not only for England, but for the world.

Pope's statement may be glancingly illuminated by a brief reference to various shifting figures of the poetic imagination. The characterizing medium of medieval literature was allegory, in which persons, animals or flowers were made to express something other, with little rights on their own; or, if they had such rights, as in Chaucer's maturity, they existed on the plane of simple realism, where things are just what they claim to be and no more, the art of the novel foreshadowed. In allegory a surface is deliberately arranged for us to see through it to a more important reality: nature may be slighted, and its laws neglected.[2] In Dante's *Divina Commedia* the human drama is ordered according to a scheme, and subordinated, with or without allegory, to meaning more important than the persons. In Shakespeare man has more rights and is, as in Pope, central, though hierarchies of natural, cosmic, and divine significance are included. A vast mass of lore, belief and observation is, far more tightly than in Spenser, crammed together, and the cramming itself witnesses to a realization of nature, man and the divine as a 'knot intrinsicate'. The separate elements are not used merely to reflect, or in any way serve, each other, nor for comparison alone; they are all but identified. At the limit, we have the human story, as in *King Lear*, becoming a universal contest; man, as in *Antony and Cleopatra*, is divinely transfigured and given, at a high moment, cosmic stature;

[1] *Horace, Ep.* I, i, 23–34.

[2] These remarks are necessarily constricted. Anyone anxious for an exact understanding of medieval allegory will turn to C. S. Lewis' *The Allegory of Love* (1936).

and his final victory becomes in *Pericles* 'the music of the spheres'. The poetry is always asserting identities, and its characteristic medium is accordingly metaphor.

Shakespeare's language is often as far from commonsense as James Joyce's. To a rational inspection it may seem to be telling a great truth, perhaps the greatest of all truths, in terms of a myriad lies. Its molten breaking down of all cultural distinctions, with nevertheless a supervening organic cohesion and a reference at every point to human affairs, is probably more mysterious than one normally supposes. It could only have happened then, and in that place; when language was in the melting-pot and where two ages met, under Elizabeth and James, in England.

Naturally enough, the contributing elements flew apart; and next we have the *striving* for the unity, as in the epic of Milton, with its titanic actions and iron will towards a synthesis never properly captured. And if we want a characterizing device, we may point to Milton's use of extended and arbitrary simile. He is, however, half in Shakespeare's world, since he develops his similes so far from their purpose that they become poems on their own, the little asides holding, for a while, as much right as the action they are supposed to serve. They are not, strictly speaking, similes at all, since the quality of likeness is not really of their essence, nor germane to the artistic purpose, which might be called atmospheric rather than elucidatory. They are really too good for what they claim to be doing, and we may be left with a grand sense of disjunction. For a more perfect use of simile as such, we must go to Dryden. We have observed how, in his task of ordering what had become an indeterminate and heterogeneous mass of thoughts and values, Dryden included pretty nearly everything whilst deeply impregnating with belief very little, if any, of it. He keeps things firmly distinguished. He can use allegory for his purpose and turn a Shakespearian metaphor; there is little he cannot do; but his finest skill is seen in his similes. His use is rational and practical. Inspect any of the similes in *All for Love* and you will find that they are far more obviously helpful than Shakespeare's clustering impressions or the Miltonic elaboration: they really do illustrate and illuminate, fitting like a glove. Their exquisite suitability derives from Dryden's critical sense of things as, normally, unlike: he has selected them with care. In Shakespeare and Milton comparisons complicate; they disturb and distend our understanding, jerk us into new modes of experience. With Dryden, they simplify and clarify, and, their work done, can be forgotten: there are no metaphysical implications. As for the famous 'conceits' of the 'metaphysicals' themselves, these appear somehow to be enjoying all the problems raised by both types of simile, whilst playing one off against the other.

And what, now, of Pope? He certainly builds on the good work of Dryden in simplifying what was in danger of overcomplication; he shares his respect for order and precision, and follows him in use of the couplet. But his field is at once less wide and more intense. He controls an, at first sight, anyway, smaller world, and yet one which reveals depth on depth of meaning. His focal centre is man; not man dramatically interlocked with a great mesh of natural and cosmic energies, as in Shakespeare; nor man and his universe torn by the 'mighty opposites' of conscience and culture, as in Milton; nor man viewed variously according to the subject, political, religious or literary, as in Dryden; but Man who in himself must achieve the synthesis or harmonization which religious and political schemes are always claiming to achieve for him, and with no great warlike or other action to assist his self-escape. Pope does not at first appear to survey all the intellectual and emotional ground covered by those others, but he covers exactly as much of it as is proper for man's task, as he saw it, of personal, civic, and religious regeneration. All the rest may, indeed, be supposed to be included, housed, in man; in individual men and women, as persons and personalities, felt as a number of most vital entities, or wholes; though these, with the society which it is their business to compose, are also felt in closest contact with those other natural and religious hierarchies which make that greater whole, the universe. Now since for all practical purposes, and Pope is very practical, the proper place for the realities shadowed by religion and philosophy is to be felt primarily within the human personality, the characterizing literary medium is, naturally enough, 'personification'.

We must avoid, for our immediate purpose, any too rigid understanding of the term. Its most obvious connotation suggests that kind of personifying of human qualities we find in the Olympian deities of Greece and Rome; and we may recall not only the great powers of ancient myth exerted on the poetry of the Augustans, but also how the noblemen of Pope's day like Lord Cobham at Stowe, whose seat Pope celebrated in one of his *Moral Essays*, loved to fill their halls and grounds with classic statuary and temples. Though they never with him became so heavy as they did later in the poetry of Gray and Collins, Pope's earlier work is sprinkled with what might be called the literary derivatives of classical mythology; that is, abstract or spiritual qualities felt as personal entities, as in

> *Black Melancholy sits, and round her throws*
> *A death-like silence, and a dead repose.*
>
> (*Eloisa to Abelard*, 165)

From this we may pass to a general use of capitalized abstract words that assume a protagonist importance, even though there be little personifying, as such:

> *All Nature is but Art, unknown to thee;*
> *All Chance, Direction which thou canst not see . . .*
>
> (*Essay on Man*, I, 289)

We meet a number of lesser abstractions, neatly used, which house emotions and values of age-old, often classic,[1] lineage, with sometimes a direct pointing to the ancients as exemplars of heroism and virtue. The valuation is, however, enlightened by a distinction of true from false heroisms that may be said to flower from Christian teaching. In *The Temple of Fame*, a poem packed with persons of classic renown, imperial war-makers get no praise:

> '*Ambitious fools!*' (*the Queen reply'd, and frown'd*)
> '*Be all your acts in dark oblivion drown'd;*
> *There sleep forgot, with mighty tyrants gone,*
> *Your statues moulder'd, and your names unknown!*'
> *A sudden cloud straight snatch'd them from my sight,*
> *And each majestic phantom sunk in night.*
>
> (350)

Pope's ease of statement derives in part from his reliance on a variety of acknowledged acceptances.[2] Fame is personified to correspond to a value Pope and his readers recognize as of high worth; 'frown'd' gathers force from a general respect to figures of authority; the threat of 'oblivion' subscribes to 'fame' as a central good; 'tyrants' avoids a difficult distinction by use of a label weighed in the balances and not

[1] For an account of the classical and Renaissance hinterland of Pope's diction see Geoffrey Tillotson, *On the Poetry of Pope* (1938), 'Language'.

[2] The general or communal qualities of eighteenth-century diction are discussed in J. R. Sutherland's *A Preface to Eighteenth Century Poetry* (1948).

found wanting throughout centuries of use; and 'statues' itself witnesses to the agreed desirability of having a statue, if at all possible. The statement's general valuation is easy enough to accept; but observe how the points made against false heroism are made in heroic, not in religious or even semi-religious, terms. When those are rejected who thought to build renown on slavery or usurpation,

Or who their glory's dire foundation lay'd
On Sov'reigns ruin'd, or on friends betray'd,

(408)

the lines speak in terms of generally accepted values of loyalty to king, country, or friend. Such a word as 'sovereigns' exists not merely as a label; it wears an aura of traditional reverence, is itself a field of semi-spiritual radiations.

But the glamour is never a false glamour, never an idolatry. The words are tested for their life, for their living and creative force, and any not ringing true will not be used. Or again, we may say that age-old and all but rigid words are rendered fluid, infused with new vitality for a subtle and highly enlightened purpose, as when the warrior imperialists are denied the fame which, one must admit, history has in fact allowed them. What Pope is doing may be best pictured in a line of his own:

Then Marble, soften'd into life, grew warm.

(*Horace, Ep.* II, i, 147)

'Marble' is an example of a concrete noun carrying a wealth of associations concerned with the Mediterranean, with architecture, with statuary. But see how this line itself dramatizes for us the process by which a first solid acceptance is made into something of human warmth. So always in Pope the word or thought of heroic pedigree is 'soften'd into life', made part of a contemporary and vital, more deeply Christian, message. Pope loves his words, his art:

This subtle Thief of life, this paltry Time,
What will it leave me if it snatch my rhyme?

(*Horace, Ep.* II, ii, 76)

The personification of Time is exquisitely set beside that other, non-temporal, possession, 'rhyme', felt with a personal, a parental or a lover's, emotion.

We may be thought to have extended the term 'personification' beyond reasonable limits; but the very extension is germane to our enquiry. Pope's words are well-chosen entities, they exist almost as little *personalities*; and this comes from their holding traditional and communal, though mainly aristocratic, associations. They are to be contrasted with the ignition-quality of metaphor; and yet, again, they are not snatched cold from the outer void of mental speculation or divine aspiration; they are warm, like a rich necklace warm from human contact. They are not clichés. A cliché is a word or phrase worn dull by vulgar use; these are words worn bright by noble use. They are valuable with the value we attach to an heirloom, or some old volume once in famous hands. In Pope's hands these words of pedigree come newly alive; if they did not, there would be no honour in their use. Both nouns and verbs have, as words, a simple, solid, yet lustrous life. It is amazing how much is done by nouns and verbs alone, and their vivid interplay within a lucid syntax sets going a continual dance: Pope's is a poetic universe alive with a myriad electronic solids. There is nothing academic, nothing static about it. If we say that his diction has 'lustre', we mean by this that it has life, like the sheen of life on a human body. Moreover, his employment of a style deriving from a rich assortment of well-chosen, well-handled and well-valued *words*, which themselves by association and heritage somehow do alone, as separate units or wholes, what is elsewhere done by metaphor, is exactly one with Pope's major statement on life; his concentration not on vast and settled, or unsettled, schemes of religion or philosophy, but rather on a world of separate, individual, free and autonomous, persons, as integral units within whom the universal purpose—for *that* is never forgotten—must be played out; and who, in their turn, are playing out their little destiny in face of a universal purpose.

But that more universal reality is not to be reached by leaping for it; it must be done through society and the nation. Pope was pre-eminently a patriot. He was associated with Bolingbroke and others who claimed the title of 'patriot', including that group of ardent young men who gathered together at Stowe under Lord Cobham, and were known as 'Cobham's cubs'.[1] Pope cannot be given a political label; and he was a poet not of war, but of peace; and yet he can be in general associated with that peculiar amalgam of aristocratic patriotism and liberal fervour which we find later in Earl

[1] See *Chatham: his Early Life and Connections*, Lord Rosebery (1910); also my account in *The Dynasty of Stowe* (1944), IV, 51–2; VI, 91; IX, 134–5.

Temple, Cobham's successor at Stowe, and in Pitt; men who willed imperial expansion, even at the cost of war, as a means to all the various arts and blessings of peace, envisaging a world close-linked by trade and freedom in a grand community preserving the heroic traditions, with peace still as a ruling concept, however strenuously to be bought.[1] Now, although Pope steered clear, except in his *Homer*, of warlike themes, his contribution as a, or rather *the*, poet of peace can only be properly assessed by realizing that peace was for him also a truly strenuous matter, demanding psychic integration and civic virtue. He is pre-eminently the poet of what Milton once, in his *Second Defence of the People of England*, called 'the campaign of peace'.[2] In this period our parliamentary system was first properly in action, and the liberties of the subject assured; and, though Pope outdistanced the best actuality of his day, as indeed a poet should, he was firmly rooted in its soil; he was not speaking to, or from, a void.

We have a graduation, as it were, from one concrete and living whole to the next; from words, concrete or abstract, nouns or verbs, to 'personification'; from 'personification' as a literary figure to dramatic entities such as the sylphs and gnomes of *The Rape of the Lock*; from these to a gallery of actual personalities, and thence to society and the nation; and finally, with no hiatus left unhealed, to the greater whole, with all its angelic and seraphic hierarchies, of the *Essay on Man*; where nevertheless the heart of its metaphysic is to be sought within the creative workshop of human personality.

Pope's diction is thus one with his general teaching; you might almost say that the teaching flowers from the diction, for his language grows plainer as his message becomes clearer. Both assert pre-eminently what might be called the *civic* virtues, his thought deriving from the city-states of those ancients whom he and Swift so deeply honoured: we have a sense of duty, honour, patriotism, just ambition, fame, nobility, and so on. Though these are interwoven with other, and more Christian, intuitions, they nevertheless take precedence over all individualistic aspirations. For Pope you

[1] As in Addison's *Royal Exchange*. See also *The Dynasty of Stowe* (1944), VII, 100–2; and *Hiroshima* (1946), II, iii, 'A New Whitehall'; and pp. 21, 23–4 below. Many of the issues involved have been discussed in Bonamy Dobrée's Warton Lecture, *The Theme of Patriotism in the Poetry of the Early Eighteenth Century* (1949); and in *The Broken Cistern* (1954).

[2] Discussed in *Chariot of Wrath* (1942), IV, 189.

feel that the highest virtue begins, like charity, at home. He is always, at the admittedly severe cost of sprinkling his page with a host of ephemeral names, calling his contemporaries back from the vast and varied speculations of the preceding century to their context as members of Augustan England, to the 'here' and 'now'. And yet that 'here' and 'now' is positively a-tingle with romantic excitement, ethical fervour, and cosmic meaning. In Pope religion and society, God and politics, spirit and body, converge. His world is compact, but burning; within its present humanity lies its eternal catholicism.

II

THE VITAL FLAME:

An Interpretative Study

II. THE VITAL FLAME[1]

I

Pope's *Pastorals*[2] (published 1709) are strikingly assured, and *Windsor Forest* (completed 1713) is a poem of first importance. Deep submission to nature is felt expanding into communal and national prophecy. The forest is a universal symbol:

Not Chaos-like together crush'd and bruis'd,
But, as the world, harmoniously confus'd:
Where order in variety we see,
And where, though all things differ, all agree.

(13)

Those four lines, balancing man and nature with feeling for an enclosing and permeating whole, are the key to Pope's work.

Descriptive phrases are often somewhat general:

Bear me, O bear me to sequester'd scenes,
The bow'ry mazes, and surrounding greens . . .

(261)

Instead of the chiselled image of Milton we have a queer refusal of visual outline, 'bow'ry mazes' being only superficially Miltonic. A quality rather than an object or set of objects is transmitted. Nor is the result necessarily vague:

There, interspers'd in lawns and op'ning glades,
Thin trees arise that shun each other's shades.

(21)

General nouns balance a vivid feeling for natural life. Notice that

[1] First published in *The Burning Oracle*, 1939.
[2] The *Pastorals* are handled below, pp. 165–7.

the personification of the trees is not a weak artifice: rather their felt stillness, their living identities, are realized. Personification in Pope is never driven to any rigid extremes. When corn is seen 'in waving prospect' (39) we have movement and a whole, steady scene, together with an abstract [1] noun: and all, movement, wholeness, and the abstract well used in service to a physical impact, are characteristic. Notice that one word describes the object, one the unifying mind of the spectator: this union is often at the back of Pope's method, as in 'quivering shade' (135), where 'shade' touches human affections. There is precision without a materialized limitation. Even when Liberty leads 'the golden years' (92), though the phrase be ornate, the expressed quality is fairly exact. In Pope any humanizing of nature is really a partnership with nature: the condensation of feeling into a choice diction that already has classic impact assists, but the feeling is always there.

Moreover, phrases do not assert themselves in isolation; a 'predominating passion' renders every image soft, one inward life warming each unit of any single description. A vital context is ready for any striking impression, as in the generally admired lines on fishes:

Our plenteous streams a various race supply,
The bright-ey'd perch with fins of Tyrian dye,
The silver eel, in shining volumes roll'd,
The yellow carp, in scales bedropp'd with gold,
Swift trouts, diversified with crimson stains,
And pikes, the tyrants of the wat'ry plains.

(141)

Here 'bright-ey'd' grades into 'silver' and 'shining', and sets a context for 'yellow', 'bedropp'd with gold', and 'crimson'.[2] There is nothing sudden or rigid; the whole movement being so organic, no complicated efforts at realization are needed; simple nouns and well-selected adjectives drop into place, and all, without strain, goes smoothly. The poet is well above his work, or rather, well inside it, or both. A lovely passage on reflections in water (212–18) pictures the miracle

[1] Geoffrey Tillotson has already drawn attention to Pope's use of abstract nouns in such phrases ('Language', 74).

[2] Pope's poetic use of *colour* has been excellently discussed by Norman Ault in *New Light on Pope* (1949). 'It would seem' he writes (v, 87), 'that Pope's conscious references to colour in *Windsor Forest* are carried to a pitch never before attained by any poet.'

of 'headlong mountains' and 'downward skies', trees that are 'absent', and 'floating forests' that 'paint the waves with green', while the water rolls 'slow' through the 'fair scene' which it holds. The description becomes a symbol of that repose mysteriously one with a vital yet undisturbing movement that characterizes Pope's major art-forms and tiniest phrases alike. The delineations, being inward, penetrate to the dynamic centres of life, and give, without effort, pictorial quality and action, as in the well-known:

See! from the brake the whirring pheasant springs,
And mounts exulting on triumphant wings:
Short is his joy; he feels the fiery wound,
Flutters in blood, and panting beats the ground.
Ah! what avail his glossy, varying dyes,
His purple crest, and scarlet-circled eyes,
The vivid green his shining plumes unfold,
His painted wings, and breast that flames with gold?

(111)

Rich as is the description, the phrases work in obedience to a whole drawn directly from the energies of nature. Each image is apt, but none superlative. There is a reserve of power and a poetic humility, power being felt in the conception, not just in the expression. The regularity of couplet-rhyme helps in checking all separate excellences, levelling and subduing them, with a corresponding release to the central experience, while poignant action informs a poetic tranquillity; as in our former phrase 'waving prospect', where the still and vast abstract conception checks the more lively movement which is somehow then enclosed in stillness. This is Keats' 'might half-slumbering on its own right arm'.

Pope's animal apprehension is one with animal sympathy. The destruction of bird-life is again vigorously imagined when a fowler is described roving with 'slaughterous gun' in winter:

He lifts the tube, and levels with his eye:
Straight a short thunder breaks the frozen sky:
Oft, as in airy rings they skim the heath,
The clam'rous lapwings feel the leaden death:
Oft, as the mounting larks their notes prepare,
They fall, and leave their little lives in air.

(129)

You could complain of 'tube', though the word may also mark an isolated visual exactitude. Pope is no specialist at mechanical imagery, and avoids it consistently. But the first couplet so precisely integrates action with atmosphere, the metallic suddenness of sound across the wintry landscape, that you almost smell powder in the keen air: a whole experience is given, an authentic instant of actual existence, a piece of a living universe. The realization is stark, sudden, and unerring; as, too, in the phrase 'leaden death'. 'Clam'rous' and 'mounting' are careful epithets, and 'little' denotes the sympathy implicit throughout, with a clever silhouetting of life's mystery in the thought of its loss, the birds as tiny flamelets puffed out in song. Animals are inwardly felt, as in the 'ready spaniel' shown 'panting with hope' (99–100) or the 'impatient courser'—'courser' because he is felt as kinetic—seen as excited in 'every vein', pawing the ground and tingling for 'the distant plain' (151). The animal's power and swiftness are admirably caught in 'earth rolls back beneath the flying steed' (158), the phrase aiming to net the paradoxical quality of speed. Animals are usually created in their vital and peculiar movement from an inward sympathy comparable with Shakespeare's, and continuous with the apprehension of dynamic quality, as well as shape and colour, in nature generally. The stallion and hare of *Venus and Adonis* are both recalled by *Windsor Forest*:

To plains with well-breath'd beagles we repair,
And trace the mazes of the circling hare:
(Beasts, urg'd by us, their fellow beasts pursue,
And learn of men each other to undo).

(121)

The animal's characterizing behaviour is noticed and exactly, though unobtrusively, recorded.

Such recognition will naturally widen beyond nature and animal life to a vivid feeling for human vitality in action, such as we find in Pan's pursuit of Lodona (171–218). A tense realization of movement and fear is projected through numerous precisions involving bird-comparisons, the sound of steps, Pan's shadow lengthened by the sun, the feeling of his very breath: it is vivid without being visual, an inward experience expressing itself freely and variously; and it should help us to understanding of Shakespeare's own similar mastery. The little drama leads up to Lodona's transmutation to a rivulet and this exquisite couplet:

The silver stream her virgin coldness keeps,
For ever murmurs and for ever weeps.

(205)

The real stream is in every accent. That process of nature-feeling which created the Greek myths, and which Keats understood so well in his own fluid personifications, enjoys an equal perfection here. The fusion of the human and the natural is not ever, in itself, a weakness; rather it is the farthest aim of all nature-mysticism. It is implicit in Wordsworth's own message.

The poem expands further, Windsor Forest becoming a national symbol, one with 'Britannia's goddess', Liberty (91). Oaks are 'future navies' (222), with no straining of association. An Elizabethan royalism is recaptured, Windsor boasting in Queen Anne 'as bright a Goddess and as chaste a Queen' as Diana in 'old Arcadia'; at once protectress of the 'sylvan scene', 'earth's fair light', and 'empress of the main' (159–64). So the courtier ranks above the poet, whose 'chymic art', reading magic lore from nature and history and associated with god-like excursions beyond earth and mortality, is a brilliantly characterized second (235–56). The Thames recalls past nobilities, river-feelings forming organically among the paradisal, yet contemporary, impressions. Again, as in the days of Elizabeth, 'discord' has been quelled, only this time by 'great Anna' (327); while the 'sacred' blessings of a peaceful reign are expected, the building of 'temples' replacing civil war and bloodshed (355–78). England is finally seen as supreme arbiter and 'great oracle' of the world (382). All evils are to be stilled on that day when

Unbounded Thames shall flow for all mankind.

(398)

The vision expands the Shakespearian prophecy in *Henry VIII*. Pope expects his country to oppose 'slavery' (408). He proclaims the end of conquest (408) and ambition (416), with the advent of universal peace.

The sense received of an organic continuity from nature, through animal-life, to human civilization, is most important. It is not a logical sequence; my quotations are drawn from various parts of what may well seem an untidy poem. The form is inherently, not studiously, organic. The generalizing tendency never loses contact with perceptual impressions. Feeling rather burrows into the underlying essence, catches the spirit and atmosphere, enjoys possession with freedom, and so moves on to the universal. The process is Shakespearian, and the final inclusion a natural result of any contact with an inner vitality. *Windsor Forest* is felt as a teeming world: there are no limits to its boundaries. We are pointed on, through thoughts of imperial expansion as creatively interlocking one's own country with a great human whole, to the 'naked youths' (405) of America; and though the positive trust in a mercantile peace, to be grouped with Addison's *Royal Exchange* and poetically forecast by the glamour of Shakespeare's merchants, is, with much else in *Windsor Forest*, superficially reversed in Pope's later writings, the essential statement of the poem is never repudiated. Evils are keenly remembered: the forest's past as a setting for savagery and oppression (43–92) is set beside its present placidity and expected future. Such Shakespearian inclusiveness, covering a number of geographical references, points towards the *Essay on Man*. Pope's life-work is rooted in *Windsor Forest*. It holds the germ of all the rest, the satires too. The ultimate significance which Milton, starting with a religious poem, searched for in the organ music of his own mind, is here again sought in natural affinities. Nature and man are again in partnership: and this recaptured harmony is reflected with an assured poetic ease into the rose-chain and bowery prison of the couplet.

II

Shakespeare gives us drama and Milton epic, and Pope builds from both in *The Rape of the Lock* (1712–14). The poem has Lyly's feeling for the delightfully evanescent, the poignant attractiveness of a brilliant society.[1] Yet Lyly offered no strong action, and against this subtlest of poetic problems Pope very early pits his genius, preserving the essence of heroic poetry on condition of a semi-humorous treatment. Attempts to idealize the crown in Dryden's *Absalom and Achitophel* are weak, and in *Windsor Forest* the national fervour barely, if at all, carries off the more royalistic idealism. But, by full acceptance of a changed mental horizon, we may regain an integrity comparable with Shakespeare's:

Here thou, great Anna! whom three realms obey,
Dost sometimes counsel take—and sometimes tea.

(III, 7)

[1] See my article on Lyly's plays in *The Review of English Studies*, April, 1939.

The compliment is made possible and even powerful by the joke. And by just such humour Pope integrates his whole poem into the heroic and religious traditions, religious tonings taking their place beside those royalistic and heroic, under similar semi-humorous conditions. The poem is not iconoclastic, but holds a warm humanism as surely as the somewhat similar *Love's Labour's Lost*. It is written not from a scorn but from a love. The whole is a flirtation with the sublime.

By seeing Belinda's toilet preparations as a ritual the poet channels reverend associations that build his scene and its action into both a more convincing and a more memorable impressionistic whole than would otherwise be possible. Nor is this merely a technical fancy, since the religion of post-Renaissance literature is, fundamentally, an Eros cult. So, in blending religious tonings with feminine vanity, Pope makes a synthesis of the Christianity-Eros conflict on a comparatively superficial, but delightfully human, plane, the rich humour being both the measure of a relation and the resolving of a conflict. Here it is:

And now, unveil'd, the Toilet stands display'd,
Each silver Vase in mystic order laid.
First, rob'd in white, the Nymph intent adores,
With head uncover'd, the Cosmetic pow'rs.
A heav'nly image in the glass appears,
To that she bends, to that her eyes she rears;
Th' inferior Priestess, at her altar's side,
Trembling begins the sacred rites of Pride.
Unnumber'd treasures ope at once, and here
The various off'rings of the world appear;
From each she nicely culls with curious toil,
And decks the Goddess with the glitt'ring spoil.
This casket India's glowing gems unlocks,
And all Arabia breathes from yonder box.
The Tortoise here and Elephant unite,
Transform'd to combs, the speckled, and the white.
Here files of pins extend their shining rows . . .

(I, 121)

He goes on to imagine a 'purer blush' suffusing her face, and 'keener lightnings' starting from her eyes. The delicate fun is obvious, but certain other significances may too easily be neglected. There is the same sense of wealth which we found in *Windsor Forest*: the poet feels his own corner of life interlocking with a vast whole of human co-operation. The use of perfumes is noteworthy: Pope consistently relies on them to establish his impressions. The whole passage is, to use the fine term applied by A. C. Bradley to the poetry of Keats, 'dense'. There is nothing visually flat. Pope is not a pre-eminently visual poet; rather he tells facts, names concrete objects, attaches needed epithets. But his reserve attains great richness, and his epithets modify with precision and force, as in the adjective 'mystic', both helping the main analogy and underlining the maid's professional care to serve a realistic purpose. The sacramental associations concretize, and give depth to, the whole business: objects are made alive, till they breathe out significant energy. Pope twice elsewhere in the poem uses such ritualistic colourings. There is the altar made of four French romances, and its offerings of love, in a passage to be quoted later, and here is a pretty description of coffee-making:

On shining Altars of Japan they raise
The silver lamp; the fiery spirits blaze:
From silver spouts the grateful liquors glide,
While China's earth receives the smoking tide.

(III, 107)

This is symbolism in a very valuable sense of the word: dynamic associations are used to realize, seriously or humorously, some whole event or scene, objects and atmosphere, facts and implications, together. Here the ordinary and trivial spring to sudden life, a hidden magic released.

Warfare, so continual in heroic, and, given a more psychological significance, in dramatic, poetry, is likewise used, twice, the one instance forming a neat forecast of the other. First, there is the card-game. The emotionally heroic treatment of it is not illogical. Games are civilized substitutes for physical rivalry, and the kings and queens in chess or cards symbolize existent meanings, an age of settled culture, as Castiglione knew, needing an outlet for its warrior instincts. So phrases such as 'now move to war her sable Matadores' (III, 47) and 'th' imperial consort of the crown of Spades' (III, 68) reflect a truth. People *do* take their games seriously; they *have* been known to lose their tempers at bridge. Remembering this, ask whether the following lines overload their context, and if the rich humour is not dependent, as finest humour should be, on the holding up of a mirror to nature:

> *And now (as oft in some distemper'd State)*
> *On one nice Trick depends the gen'ral fate.*
> *An Ace of Hearts steps forth: the King unseen*
> *Lurk'd in her hand, and mourn'd his captive Queen:*
> *He springs to Vengeance with an eager pace,*
> *And falls like thunder on the prostrate Ace.*
> *The nymph exulting fills with shouts the sky;*
> *The wells, the woods, and long canals reply.*
>
> (III, 93)

The ordinary word 'thunder', without any attempt at original phrase-coining, starts from its context with crashing impact; next, the movement curves over to the quiet end of a completed whole, the usual Shakespearian technique in the organizing of speech, scene, or play. The rich humour is proportional to our recognition not of a distortion but of a truth, depending, indeed, on a central, Shakespearian, humility before the simple and the vast in human instincts. It is a quality which tends to elude the puritanical consciousness.

Our other war-incident is the general mêlée in Canto V. Though feminine dignity may be for a while lost as 'whalebones crack' (v. 40), it is often cleverly preserved in delightfully mock-heroic terms, as when Thalestris 'scatters death around from both her eyes' (v. 58), or Belinda scores a victory with a charge of snuff thrown at the Baron till 'the high dome re-echoes to his nose' (v. 86). There is, too, the Shakespearian realization of personal dignity where you least expect it, in the brainless aristocrat Sir Plume, with 'earnest eyes and round unthinking face', who has nevertheless also the mystery of his own precise individuality, and therefore his own causes of pride:

> *Sir Plume of amber snuff-box justly vain,*
> *And the nice conduct of a clouded cane.*
>
> (IV, 123)

The persons, it is true, are not strongly individualized except for this exquisite vignette of Sir Plume and his cleverly characterized words, but the presentation of people in general has a warmth, conviction, and sympathy that might well, at another time, have created drama on a wider scale. The fun is not derisive but cathartic.

Pope's use of his supernatural 'machinery' is clever. These 'light Militia of the lower sky' (I, 42; observe the skilful 'i'-sounds) increase dramatic suspense, and therefore story-depth, since they foreknow and warn of the central disaster; help to universalize semi-humorously the whole action, used neatly as the binding symbolism of the little drama; are related to certain paradisal and, in Umbriel's journey, hellish colourings touching Dante, Shakespeare, and Milton; and finally reflect the implied belief of poetic art-forms in general that humanity and its sensible world do not exhaust the total of a comprehensive statement. They are of a race that lives in the pure upper light, that guides 'orbs' in heaven, like the child-spirit in Shelley's *Prometheus Unbound*, and follows shooting stars by moonlight. They are variously associated with rainbow, mists, tempests, earth, and the guardianship of the British throne (II, 77–90). They are explicitly related to traditional beliefs, both trivial and profound:

Fairest of mortals, thou distinguish'd care
Of thousand bright Inhabitants of Air!
If e'er one vision touch'd thy infant thought,
Of all the Nurse and all the Priest have taught;
Of airy elves by moonlight shadows seen,
The silver token, and the circled green,
Or virgins visited by Angel-pow'rs,
With golden crowns and wreaths of heav'nly flow'rs . . .

(I, 27)

They are also spirits of the dead, now acting as guardian angels to the living (I, 47–66). They are in part quite seriously imagined, and exquisitely realized, with names delicately composed to suit their peculiar charges; Zephyretta, Brillante, Momentilla, Crispissa corresponding to fan, drops, watch, and lock. Nowhere is Pope's artistry in vowel-colour more evident than in the description of Belinda's setting out on the Thames by sunlight with sylphs invisibly attending. The passage is introduced by three lines of light 'i'-sounds, followed by weightier though soft vowellings to match the expansive peace:

But now secure the painted vessel glides,
The sun-beams trembling on the floating tides:
While melting music steals upon the sky,

And soften'd sounds along the waters die;
Smooth flow the waves, the Zephyrs gently play,
Belinda smiled, and all the world was gay.

(II, 47)

Soon after, the Sylphs' introduction is accompanied by a growing accumulation of 'i' vowels, steadily increasing in clustered force for eight lines, before giving place to heavier sounds:

Some to the sun their insect-wings unfold,
Waft on the breeze, or sink in clouds of gold;
Transparent forms, too fine for mortal sight,
Their fluid bodies half dissolv'd in light,
Loose to the wind their airy garments flew,
Thin glitt'ring textures of the filmy dew,
Dipt in the richest tincture of the skies,
Where light disports in ever-mingling dyes,
While ev'ry beam new transient colours flings,
Colours that change whene'er they wave their wings.
Amid the circle, on the gilded mast,
Superior by the head, was Ariel plac'd;
His purple pinions op'ning to the sun,
He rais'd his azure wand, and thus begun . . .

(II, 59)

In the couplet starting 'While every . . .' heavy and light sounds interpenetrate to match the formation of deep colours from out aerial brilliance.[1] Continual change and motion are cleverly expressed in a various dance of evanescent impressions very different from Milton's more static, or at the best solemn, appeals. The final lines grow thicker with vowel-weight to establish a mock-heroic grandeur and cause the little speaker to swell out in close-up significance. So delicately rich and substantial an impressionism cannot be exhausted by categories of social satire: you could seriously compare this river-and-lady sun-piece with Shakespeare's Cleopatra on Cydnus. The description, as 'insect-wings' implies, depends on a close observation of nature. Pope's sympathy with small life-forms is

[1] In her 'Notes on Pope's Poetry', Edith Sitwell has commented on the 'texture' of this passage. She regards lines 59–68 as a crystallization of the poem's unique quality (*Alexander Pope*, 1930; XVIII, 272–3).

continual, and leads here to an exquisite apprehension of a sylph's (or fly's) punishment:

Gums and pomatums shall his flight restrain,
While clogg'd he beats his silken wings in vain.

(II, 129)

Heavy vowels oppose light ones. Later (II, 135) there is the horror and rounded sounds of 'fumes of burning Chocolate'. Triumphant Umbriel—another exquisite name—is shown mischievously clapping his wings 'on a sconce's height' during the mêlée (V, 54), and the sombre effects of his descent to Hell, with comic description of the objects there, are done with a glorious sense of the trivial sublimated to heroic stature. The dark and light tonings throughout expand far beyond 'mockery'; rather the humour is the condition of poetic achievement.

The poem has imaginative solidity, which is not the same as the imagining of solids in separation, presenting perceptual density and a close-packed unity. I have noticed the perceptual quality of Belinda's toilet, but, whatever is handled, the Lock itself, the guarded petticoat, Sir Plume's 'amber snuff-box' and 'clouded cane', bodkins, sconces, coffee-pots, all are rounded and convincing, and cohere together in their particular world. There is a heavy stress on bright substances, which are here peculiarly fitting. Silver is a persistent impression: 'The press'd watch return'd a silver sound' (I, 18), a 'silver token' (I, 32), 'each silver vase' (I, 122), the 'silver Thames' (II, iv), the petticoat's 'silver bound' (II, 121), the 'silver lamp' and 'silver spouts' of coffee-pots (III, 108–9). There is gold too: angels with 'golden crowns' (I, 34), 'golden scales' (V, 71), 'liquid gold' (IV, 45) in the Cave of Spleen, 'clouds of gold' (II, 60). It may take the form of gilt: 'gilded chariots' (I, 55), the 'gilded mast' (II, 69), the French romances 'neatly gilt' (II, 38). But these rich solids—there are jewels too—blend naturally into the silvery glinting wings of sylphs in sunlight, the recurrent 'i'-sounds, the 'lightning' of Belinda's sparkling eyes (I, 144), the glitter of poetic wit. Belinda dreams of 'a youth more glitt'ring than a birth-night beau' (I, 23), her jewellery is a 'glitt'ring spoil' (I, 132), the scissors to cut the lock a 'glitt'ring forfex' (III, 147). Over all is raised the Lock, itself finally carried with a 'radiant trail' of light (V, 128) to 'bespangle' the heavens. These impressions are gained almost entirely by naming appropriate objects; there is no over-plastering of descriptive imagery; nor is the aggregate result itself metallic, but rather warm with human contact, the prevailing impression being one of softness. Moreover, that most poignant method of bodying out the subtly atmospheric into poetic solidity, the use of smell, assists in 'Arabia' breathing from a box (I, 134), the 'imprison'd essences' (II, 94), and the 'fragrant steams' (III, 134) of coffee. A profoundly sensuous nature is creating.

Though the humour is never bitterly satiric, Pope does sometimes appear as an amused grown-up writing of children; but then each of us is a grown-up, and the rest all children, where romantic emotions are concerned. So we get a delicate treatment of girls' amours with suggestion that the Gnomes

Teach Infant-cheeks a bidden blush to know,
And little hearts to flutter at a Beau.

(I, 89)

A strangely purified sexuality is attained by this blend of child-innocence and desire, as in Byron's *Don Juan*. There is, as it were, a love for the object's very littleness, recalling the larks of *Windsor Forest* and the creation of the Sylphs themselves. The Sylphs protect young ladies from unchastity, by keeping their attention on the move:

When Florio speaks what virgin could withstand,
If gentle Damon did not squeeze her hand?
With varying vanities, from ev'ry part,
They shift the moving Toyshop of their heart.

(I, 97)

Though lightly, a deep enough human truth is hinted. The gentle mockery may be yet deeper, as in

What guards the purity of melting Maids,
In courtly balls, and midnight masquerades,
Safe from the treach'rous friend, the daring spark,
The glance by day, the whisper in the dark,
When kind occasion prompts their warm desires,
When music softens, and when dancing fires?

(I, 71)

It is the Sylphs who mysteriously save them, functioning as does the Attendant Spirit of *Comus*, and corresponding to what psychologists, who may not believe in such spirits, call 'inhibitions'. Notice especially the warm, sensuous creation here, the exquisite subtlety of verbal tone, consonants and vowels variously inter-shading.

In this last passage we may observe the central pauses in lines 2, 3, 4 and 6, and their comparative absence in lines 1 and 5. Such significant interplay is constant throughout Pope and should be carefully watched and followed in reading. Often contrasts are neatly balanced within one line. Here is another good example, where the antithesis of lines 1 and 2 with no internal pauses speeds up to internal antithesis in 3 and 4, gathers into the tripartite formation of line 5, and ends with a falling, run-on, pauseless unit in line 6:

Whether the nymph shall break Diana's law,
Or some frail China jar receive a flaw;
Or stain her honour, / or her new brocade;
Forget her pray'rs, / or miss a masquerade;
Or lose her heart, / or necklace, / at a ball;
Or whether Heav'n has doom'd that Shock must fall.

(II, 105)

The contrasts of the important and the trivial are vitally organic, one at least definitely balancing flirtation and religion, playing on the usual conflict. The use of caesura is interesting: often you have in reading to change your vocal colour, and even pace, in mid-line. Here pauses hold up the speed for couplet after couplet, with a final swift release, and run-on. You find something similar in Virgil, and my understanding has been assisted by my brother's study of Virgilian verse-groups,[1] from which I take the term 'release'. Other variations are employed. You can discover them by reading aloud, often altering the pace and vocal colour in mid-line, with close attention to the stops, commas especially, which are carefully placed. Striking subtleties will reveal themselves. You must, however, never ignore the couplet basis and its rhymes, since only in close reference to these do the variations hold their value.

The love-feeling, the erotic warmth, is at once soft and burning, while the poetic medium attains a perfect poise of relaxation and control. The society Pope writes of is felt as eminently desirable. We may be amused at the Baron who builds an altar to love of 'twelve vast French romances neatly gilt' and lays on it

. . . three garters, half a pair of gloves;
And all the trophies of his former loves.

(II, 39)

[1] *Accentual Symmetry in Virgil* by W. F. Jackson Knight (1939).

Yet when Belinda's toilet is seen as a 'holy ritual' and her lock called 'sacred', it is not all comedy. She presides over the poem, with an especially spirited attraction:

Her lively looks a sprightly mind disclose,
Quick as her eyes, and as unfix'd as those:
Favours to none, to all she smiles extends;
Oft she rejects, but never once offends.

(II, 9)

Such is the vital centre of Pope's inspiration: Shakespeare's Rosalind might be so described, or Portia; they, too, are felt as all but divine, without losing humanity. Pope writes from a half-feminine gentleness, and can create sunshine feminine vitality from loving admiration. His light, humorous touch continually blends, as Milton, except once in Eden, cannot or must not, romantic and religious emotions; and so, in terms precisely suited to this glittering world, he sets on his heroine's 'white breast' a 'sparkling cross' (II, 7).

The manipulation of the action as a whole is dramatic rather than epic; and here, if we remember the comparative failure of long narrative in *The Faery Queen* and *Paradise Lost*, we may consider Pope's judgement sound. The excitement may be of a sort often found in epic, as at the vividly presented climax:

Swift to the Lock a thousand Sprites repair,
A thousand wings, by turns, blow back the hair;
And thrice they twitch'd the diamond in her ear;
Thrice she look'd back, and thrice the foe drew near . . .

(III, 135)

But this rises from a dramatically conceived whole, with Shakespearian forewarnings and fears. After the central event, the held-up suspense finds violent release in discordant passions and Umbriel's visit to the Cave of Spleen, as though a glittering outside had been shattered to disclose gloom; but there is a return to sympathy, dignity, and an almost tragic pathos. The poem is close knit, with a dominating central climax and a curve over, more like a Shakespearian play than any epic, and it concludes on a note of quiet power.

A deeper note is struck towards the end. Clarissa urges that women should be gentle, not angry, else 'why Angels call'd and Angel-like adored?' (V, 12). The thought recalls similar speeches at the conclusions of *The Taming of the Shrew* and *Love's Labour's Lost*, where ill moods and superficial glitter are respectively reminded of the tragic undertones of human existence. She continues:

Oh! if to dance all night, and dress all day,
Charm'd the small-pox, or chas'd old age away . . .

(v, 19)

—then, she says, gaiety alone might be our guiding star:

But since, alas! frail beauty must decay,
Curl'd or uncurl'd, since Locks will turn to grey . . .

(v, 25)

Read the last line slowly, dwelling on the vowels and wistfully stressing 'will'. Pope's profound treatment of superficiality is to be rigidly distinguished from the more facile, and more usual, brilliance of a superficial treatment of human profundities. No poem ever had a more exquisitely sensitive introduction than that addressed to Miss Arabella Fermor, nor any ended with so sure and sweet a pathos that, in placing the heroine's beauty in a context of ultimate defeat, somehow crowns it with an immortal lustre. The poet imagines the Lock lifted as a starry constellation, which is also the constellation of his poem, glittering through the centuries:

Not all the tresses that fair head can boast,
Shall draw such envy as the Lock you lost.
For, after all the murders of your eye,
When, after millions slain, yourself shall die:
When those fair suns shall set, as set they must,
And all those tresses shall be laid in dust,
The Lock the Muse shall consecrate to fame,
And 'midst the stars inscribe Belinda's name.

(v, 143)

'Consecrate': notice again the sacred and ritualistic colouring. Reading, let the commas hold up the movement with positionally varied pauses, changing your vocal colour deeply for 'as set they must', till in line 6 there is a quick release; then let the last couplet go with stately, measured emphasis. Again, notice the verbal statement and the concrete nouns. Though there is deepest sympathy, emotion never overspills the control; you read from a height, with sense of a unit completed at each instant, though each couplet is also organic to the paragraph whole. His 'holistic' instinct is at the back of Pope's allegiance to the couplet.

A synthesis of the sexual and the religious is organic to the humour of *The Rape of the Lock*. The depths lightly tinted there are more richly blended in *Eloisa to Abelard* (1717), where the same balance assumes a poignant emotional and tragic force. This is certainly Pope's greatest human poem, and probably the greatest short love poem in our language. Pope's early development is peculiarly Elizabethan: from the idyllic nature of the *Pastorals* to the blend of rustic idealism and national vigour in *Windsor Forest*, through the scintillating and courtly, yet never superficially 'witty', *Rape of the Lock*, itself, like Shakespeare's comedies, showing deep tragic relations; and so on to the tragic music of *Eloisa to Abelard*.

Religion is early impregnated with sombre tonings:

In these deep solitudes and awful cells,
Where heav'nly-pensive contemplation dwells,
And ever-musing melancholy reigns;
What means this tumult in a Vestal's veins?

(1)

Its sanctity is imbued with a Websterian grimness and pallor:

Relentless walls! whose darksome round contains
Repentant sighs, and voluntary pains:
Ye rugged rocks! which holy knees have worn;
Ye grots and caverns shagg'd with horrid thorn!
Shrines! where their vigils pale-eye'd virgins keep,
And pitying saints, whose statues learn to weep . . .

(17)

Remorseless repetition and craggy consonants first toll the eternal sameness, rising to the thin tortured vowels of the last line but one. The nunnery is an old Websterian building, almost, you feel, a ruin, like Byron's Norman Abbey, whose 'moss-grown domes' and 'awful arches' (142–3) make of noon an eternal night, and whose 'dim windows', reversing the Miltonic pleasure, shed a grave-like calm (144). Watch now for the darkly rich vowel-colourings and held-up movement of this speech of death:

But o'er the twilight groves, / and dusky caves,
Long-sounding aisles, / and intermingled graves,

Black Melancholy sits, / and round her throws
A death-like silence, / and a dead repose:
Her gloomy presence / saddens all the scene,
Shades every flow'r, / and darkens ev'ry green,
Deepens the murmur / of the falling floods,
And breathes a browner horror on the woods.

(163)

My reading is as I have marked. The five strong internal pauses occur naturally where our text uses commas: the use is precise. Other internal pauses are slighter, and the last line shows a release, the assonance and close epithetical union of 'browner' and 'horror' forcing, I think, the run-on. Pope's full-throated mastery of vowel-colour is rich as Keats' when he needs it. Both favour a subtle interplay of light and shade, often a dark richness atmospherically suggesting woodland depths, with the same sacramental vowellings of emotions grave yet lovely. Both project the numinous and atmospheric through heavy sensuous perception, as many trees making one woodland company. Milton's exquisite, and, indeed, often Keatsian, solids are rarely so subdued, though his work was, no doubt, a most generous assistance to Pope. See again this labouring movement:

When round some mould'ring tow'r pale ivy creeps,
And low-brow'd rocks hang nodding o'er the deeps.

(243)

Nature is here part of a mood, one with an emotion. The created whole has a mysterious life Milton's grouped individual excellences do not normally attain, Pope's nature-paragraphs cohering to build a living, semi-human presence. Here a deathly stillness is required, but he was equally at home with the vital movement and sun-sparkling gaiety of *The Rape of the Lock*.

From this world of Websterian ruin and forbidding death Eloisa asserts poignantly her own, natural, desire:

Tho' cold like you, unmov'd and silent grown,
I have not yet forgot myself to stone.
All is not Heav'n's while Abelard has part,
Still rebel nature holds out half my heart.

(23)

The use of ruins, statues, and here 'stone' to build a specifically religious eternity in contrast with love exactly resembles Byron's in *Don Juan*. Eloisa accuses religion of killing those 'best of passions', love and fame, the erotic and power instincts, ideals of emotion and action. Married love she is proud of having refused, despising any such compact: 'Curse on all laws but those which love has made.' Honour and respect are nothing in comparison with so jealous a god. If the other God offered her Himself and the whole Creation, she would 'scorn 'em all'; would rather be a 'mistress' to the man she loves than a Caesar's empress (73–90). She aspires to absolute unmoral freedom in love's bondage. Yet this sin-tormented desire is close to Dante's, and also Milton's, Paradise:

> *Oh! happy state! when souls each other draw,*
> *When love is liberty, and nature law.*
>
> (91)

But neither Dante nor Milton would dare a dramatic sympathy to Eloisa's over-leaping of moral canons in order to get there; and yet this imaginative willingness is precisely the condition of Pope's advance to the poetic stature of *Antony and Cleopatra* and *Don Juan*; a symptom, we can call it, of his clear, objective, ordering of emotions. Milton's ethical sense in *Comus* attempts a premature and disrupting resolution where Pope allows full speech to the opposing principles. When Eloisa, nearing the 'dread altars', made her final vows, her eyes were fixed, not on the Cross, but on Abelard (115–16). He is, to her, Christ. Sin or god, he remains 'delicious poison' (122), an 'unholy joy' (224). Her reason is shown as unable to fight her whole life, of which it is itself a part, a thought pointing on to the more explicit psychology of the *Essay on Man*. Desire she may conquer by day, but in sleep, when 'nature' is 'free'—and what power lies in this easy expression of a simple yet terrifying thought —it rises newly strong and unconquerable; for then 'all my loose soul unbounded springs to thee' (225–8). There is here more of a Byronic sin-sense in the protagonist than in *Antony and Cleopatra*: 'glowing guilt' itself 'exalts the keen delight' (230). But there is no imaginative confusion, however complex the issues, nor any pronouncing of judgement. It is interesting to find so Shakespearian an artist clarifying objectively the experience of sin *increasing* delight on so high a plane, since this it is which so troubles Spenser and Milton, and which Shakespeare leaves almost untouched, except perhaps in Angelo, or the imaginative texture, as distinct from the persons, of *Antony and Cleopatra*; though, to be sure, Eloisa's 'delicious poison' was first spoken by Cleopatra of Antony. In her dream every 'source of love' is alive, she sees Abelard vividly present: 'I hear thee, see thee, gaze o'er all thy charms' (232–3); only to wake, phantom-deceived.

But from this burning conflict serene poetry may build in piling couplets a massed movement crowning human instinct with accomplished and inevitable victory:

I waste the Matin lamp in sighs for thee,
Thy image steals between my God and me,
Thy voice I seem in ev'ry hymn to hear,
With ev'ry bead I drop too soft a tear.
When from the censer clouds of fragrance roll,
And swelling organs lift the rising soul,
One thought of thee puts all the pomp to flight,
Priests, tapers, temples, swim before my sight:
In seas of flame my plunging soul is drown'd,
While Altars blaze, and Angels tremble round.

(267)

Never is Pope happier than when writing in terms of ritual. Here read the first four lines quietly, but let sound a heavier note thereafter. Notice the reliance on smell in the 'fragrance' of incense, and how the organ grandeur and the weighty nouns of sacred reference find each their place but no more, showing an effortless control of the magnificent comparable with Milton's, though less assertive than his, since no grandest part stifles, even for an instant, the breathing life of the whole unit. All dissolves into that whole, Abelard and Eloisa too, into a burning yet concrete whole, a human blaze that is its own flame-tipped altar, till angels themselves tremble at the might of a human sanctity. The crystallization and solidity of indefinable experience are throughout the passage maintained, to give us a rounded and an effortless perfection, mastering and liberating the whole statement. This is an embodiment of Keats' counsel to surprise 'by a fine excess', though one, paradoxically, subdued to the whole movement always, as Keats, too, surely intended; his 'might half-slumbering on its own right arm', his rise and sunset fall of image.[1] Pope, as surely as any English writer, in his best work in

[1] To Taylor, 27 Feb., 1818; *Sleep and Poetry*, 237.

this kind, loads 'every rift with ore'.[1] You need to weigh every word in turn: how easy it is, for example, to miss here the terrific force in the admirably placed word 'plunging'.

Abelard is thus, to Eloisa, all but the divine, his voice heard in the hymn, his presence obscuring, replacing, God's, so that the opposition almost becomes a synthesis. Elsewhere, starting from the divine, we are made to imagine a blessed sanctity enclosing all human richness. Here it is, the other, and yet not dissimilar, synthesis, starting not from 'nature' but from 'grace', to use the terms of Pope's preliminary note. Eloisa describes the saintly life:

Desires compos'd, affections ever ev'n;
Tears that delight, and sighs that waft to heav'n.
Grace shines around her with serenest beams,
And whisp'ring Angels prompt her golden dreams.
For her th' unfading rose of Eden blooms,
And wings of Seraphs shed divine perfumes,
For her the Spouse prepares the bridal ring,
For her white virgins Hymenaeals sing,
To sounds of heavenly harps she dies away,
And melts in visions of eternal day.

(213)

'Melts': the warm sensuousness which we noted in *The Rape of the Lock*—'melting maids' and 'midnight masquerades'—here impregnates the divine with marriage-symbolism. Remember the earlier, erotic, phrase 'when music softens' (p. 29): here is the heavenly softness, 'wafts' at the start, 'melts' at the close, and, between, 'whisp'ring', 'rose', 'Hymenaeals', with numerous 'f's and 'v's. Again, observe the 'perfumes'. The lines are best given a slight midway pause until a delicate run-on for the last. Pope's angels, seraphs, altars, incense, all are vital beyond those of other English poets. They are sensuously felt, but the softness never becomes a total relaxation: the poetry controls its own sensuous abandon, at every instant objectifies and projects the dissolving subjectivity, crystallizing a melting emotion into verbal weight.

Pope is Dantesque, yet perhaps more human, to us, than Dante. There is no rigid line of demarcation to be drawn between his seraphs and delightful sylphs: his mind is all of a piece, his poetic world, nor only in this period, a single whole.

[1] Keats to Shelley, August, 1820.

About to surrender to this dream of the divine, Eloisa again rebels, crying, in the manner of Drayton's sonnet, even while 'dawning grace' is 'opening' on her soul:

Come, if thou dar'st, all charming as thou art!
Oppose thyself to heav'n; dispute my heart . . .

(281)

'Penitence and prayers' are 'fruitless'. Therefore

Snatch me, just mounting, from the blest abode;
Assist the fiends and tear me from my God!

(287)

I do not think another example in English of this recurring conflict strikes so shivering a climax. Notice the hampering pauses, aiding the sense, and how that last line of unsurpassed, perhaps unequalled, force is done almost entirely by plain concrete nouns and active verbs.

The general effect is one of sharp, agonizing conflict tragically resolved; though it is a conflict aspiring to a blend, as we have seen, since nature touches, or rather overwhelms, grace at one point, and grace absorbs nature at another. We who read feel a resolution Eloisa cannot be supposed to know. A vast nature broods over the whole: the dark eternity was from the start imagined largely in natural terms, and the conflict is unobtrusively related to tempests, seas, and winds. There is also a kindlier nature-imagery, of pines, wandering streams, and lakes that 'quiver' in the breeze (155–60); and a calm sea (253). The poem's end is calm. Abelard from the start is 'mixed' in Eloisa's mind with the image of God (12); he seemed 'angelic', as some 'emanation from th' all-beauteous Mind' (61–2), but she loves him as a 'man', not an 'angel', envying no 'joys of saints', nor any heaven in exchange for love (70–2). There is one resolution only wherein the divine hymenaeals will be one with the human: death, where frailties fall away, and it will be no longer sin to 'mix' with Abelard (176). A voice speaks to her, as she rests 'on some tomb, a neighbour of the dead' (304), and one who had suffered likewise calls her to peace. Is that peace a living heaven or an everlasting night? We are told:

. . . All is calm in this eternal sleep;
Here grief forgets to groan, and love to weep.

(313)

And yet she who speaks is a living, 'sainted', maid. Anyway, in death God absolves all 'frailties'. So now Eloisa would die, with Abelard, in 'sacred vestments' and with 'hallow'd taper', presenting the Cross to her eyes, to symbolize the transition from lover to Christ (325–7). At this last moment, when tragic serenity holds all in a final union, comes that last withering bitterness, which is yet no bitterness but another blessedness, a paradox revolving on the very axis of death's mystery. Eloisa is dead. Let Abelard come:

Ah then, thy once-lov'd Eloisa see!
It will be then no crime to gaze on me.

(329)

And yet, again, death 'all eloquent' proves 'what dust we dote on when 'tis man we love' (336). Death's very negation is a voice, a statement.

Heavenly love resembles Abelard's (342). Abelard, Christ, Death, each is all at the last, confusedly, mystically. But the whole poem is its own only answer. Our earlier passage of love's victorious powers must be felt as complementary to the Dantesque paradise, and both related to the conclusion. The unity within and controlling the conflict is remarkable, the very agony creating resolution before our eyes, nature and grace being felt as one at the sharpest moment of dispute. The more forceful the emotion, the more serene the poet's mastery. Certain couplet paragraphs attain to intense and well-varied dramatic expression, with a natural, almost Shakespearian, coherence and rhythmic subtlety; [1] others, as we have seen, build separate excellences of sensuous warmth. The poem is strangely serene. Its emotional structures form and dissolve, it lives with a softly beating movement, glowing and fading, like the pulsing of a star.

III

Superficial differences should not prevent our recognizing the Shakespearian affinities of Pope's first period in subject, emotional sympathy, and general control. His verse technique itself derives ultimately, it would seem, from Iago's speech to Desdemona after

[1] Our relegation of Pope's poetry to silent study has done it a grave injustice. Given an adequate vocal projection, with full attention to modulation of vowel colour and variation in pace and pause, *Eloisa to Abelard* will be found as powerful a dramatic monologue as any in our literature.

their landing at Cyprus, variations of a similar sort being woven across a similar regularity of couplet and caesura.[1] Therefore his two more philosophical poems, his *Essay on Criticism* and *Essay on Man*, can be supposed to reflect not only his own views on literature and life, but some part also of Shakespeare's; there is, probably, no nearer analogy. Although the two poems were written at different periods, the first when Pope was only twenty, they develop a single, coherent, argument. Pope resembles Shakespeare and Milton in his straight-line development, his axes of reference being the same from first to last. These concern (i) nature, and (ii) a sense of the whole; together with a heavy stress on pride as the main hindrance to creative understanding. I offer next, with apologies for what I none the less feel to be necessary and unavoidable, brief abstracts of the two poems.

The *Essay on Criticism* (1711) is strikingly relevant today, though it is, unfortunately, only too easy to let Pope's trenchant exposition pass over the surface of one's understanding. The argument is often challenging, and many of his points, if offered now, might incur the charge of an excessive romanticism.

The critical intelligence is severely handled. Let those censure, we are told, who can write themselves; 'false learning' has damaged good sense; much poor criticism derives from inferiority and jealousy. Pope's centre of operation is an implanted faith in 'unerring nature': that is, creative life. This is the 'source', 'end', and 'test' of all art. Nature always 'works without show and without pomp presides', which is true enough of Pope's work, but less so of Milton's; it informs the whole organism as 'soul' a living 'body'; 'unseen', it yet imparts vitality to all else. But instinctive power is not by itself enough. 'Wit' (i.e. native ability) needs the control of judgement, and the two should work in harmony: ''Tis more to guide than spur the muses' steed.' Nevertheless, nature remains primary and is only restrained, as Shakespeare's Polixenes also tells us, by laws of her own making, critical precepts coming, not from man's reason, but from Heaven: that is, nature in its widest sense (68–99). Too often critics, being creative failures themselves, seize on rules easy to understand,

[1] This has been remarked by Geoffrey Tillotson, and by someone else earlier, though who it was I cannot recall. I am not, of course, denying the vast difference between Pope and Shakespeare in terms of period and taste, and for a valuable side-light on this difference would point to John Butt's *Pope's Taste in Shakespeare* (1936).

pronounce judgement on their betters, and 'write dull receits how poems should be made'. If you should respect Homer, that is merely because Homer—we today might add Shakespeare—introduces you direct to nature. But no 'rules' are absolute; there is a 'grace beyond the reach of art' and any licence that works is itself a 'rule'. Rules are aids to expression, not limitations of it, and the end, not the means, is important (105–180).

Pride blurs understanding and leads to folly, but, pride once banished, 'truth breaks upon us with resistless day' (201–12). That is, many universal truths which cannot be positively demonstrated are self-evident once certain rigid mental hindrances related to intellectual pride are removed. Truth is in this way almost a moral quality. The thought relates to the New Testament and Pope's own *Essay on Man* very closely. Much faulty criticism, we may suggest, is due to the critic's not being able to conceive that a writer has touched an apprehension beyond his own, and a consequent unconscious abstracting of what he himself can most easily receive, the usual stressing of Perdita to the neglect of the Hermione-resurrection in *The Winter's Tale* being a modern instance. Which leads us to Pope's next point.

The art-form must be understood in the spirit of its composition and seen, or felt, as a *whole*. If it is vitalized by 'nature' and warmed by feeling, 'slight faults' are irrelevant. Cold correctness is not art. Parts, as parts, do not count in themselves, any more than a 'lip' or an 'eye' can make human beauty. Therefore no single element should obtrude overmuch. But critics, too often themselves 'fond of some subservient art' (e.g.—as we may suggest—history, theology, economics, biography, stage-technique, psychology, or indeed literary criticism—or interpretation—itself), some private interest of their own, 'still make the Whole depend upon a Part' (233–66). This continual doctrine of the whole is, of course, complementary to Pope's emphasis on a central life-force, 'nature', with derogatory remarks concerning the 'false learning' (19–27) of critics: since, as Pope observes, it is the unifying life that makes any whole organic. As a corollary, it follows that excessive ornament and verbosity are bad, departing from nature, that is, from sincerity: we may remember Pope's own instinctive reliance on nouns and verbs. Too much concentration on 'language' is bad; originality is as dangerous a temptation as copying; avoid 'laboured nothings' (289–336).

Critics who think only of surface smoothness and metrical delight miss many more important substances:

> *In the bright Muse though thousand charms conspire,*
> *Her voice is all these tuneful fools admire.*
>
> (339)

Notice the word 'thousand'. That is, they miss the statement of the whole comprised, we may add, of sense-suggestion, subtle associations, ideas and symbols of all sorts, and much else; so dissolving it away into metrical and verbal technique, as people go to church for the music rather than the doctrine and substance. Literary cliques, we are told, are a danger, since 'wit' (i.e. poetic talent) becomes the supposed possession of a few with the rest damned. Do not ask whether a work be new or old: ask only if it be true. Critics who judge an author according to his personal importance rather than his works are a 'servile herd'. The vulgar err by imitation, the learned by a forced, inorganic, originality; rather than follow the crowd they 'purposely go wrong' (394–429). Praise is of little value that waits till others approve (474–5). A critic should preserve humanity and good sense: if all 'seems infected', the disease may be not in the object, but in the critic's own eye (558–9). Right criticism is as much a matter of moral fibre as of learning, and true counsel is not effective unless offered with tact (560–77). Pope's emphasis is everywhere *vital*. Every point scores, though I doubt if the last caution is sufficiently observed in such lines as:

> *The bookful blockhead, ignorantly read,*
> *With loads of learned lumber in his head . . .*
>
> (612)

In Horace cool judgement was one with poetic inspiration, whereas today, says Pope, the reverse holds: critics judge violently, but write weakly.

The contemporary challenge to us is obvious. A creative intelligence opposes the academic and formalized mind. It is the old unfortunate opposition of the New Testament and it seems impossible to advance, though some good might come of attending to Pope's own clarifying of the issue in terms of two specific concepts: (i) nature, or vital power, and (ii) the whole. These may be considered respectively centre and circumference of Pope's universe. It is clear why 'the last and greatest Art' is the 'Art to blot',[1] since concern for the whole organism must sometimes involve the removal of some cancerous growth, itself aspiring to an independent, and therefore hostile, organic life of its own; like Milton's Satan, though we can be heartily glad of the fault. 'Nature' and 'judgement', power and control, instinct and art, may be unified under the holistic concept, since control of any part is constituent to the organic quality of a whole existing, as an organism, through the infusing power of its own central, and instinctive, life. Control acts in service to nature, not to dominate it, as Pope clearly asserts, and his own paragraph-units illustrate the maxim.

The *Essay on Man* (1733–4) is a precise development of the same doctrine on a wider front. It is not only a poetic philosophy, but the universal philosophy, not so much of poets as of poetry; and is, exactly, the philosophy implied by Shakespeare's work. Epistle II starts with a reaction from Milton ('presume not God to scan'), the more clear from the earlier claim (I, 16) to 'vindicate' instead of 'justify' His ways.[2] Pope still stresses the whole, nature, and the opacities of pride.

In the first Epistle our attention is drawn early to the vast cosmic whole, a 'mighty maze, but not without a plan', recalling *Windsor Forest*. To criticize it from the limitations of human reason is absurd:

He, who thro' vast immensity can pierce,
See worlds on worlds compose one universe,
Observe how system into system runs,
What other planets circle other suns,
What vary'd Being peoples ev'ry star,
May tell why Heav'n has made us as we are.
But of this frame the bearings, and the ties,
The strong connexions, nice dependencies,
Gradations just, has thy pervading soul
Look'd thro'? or can a part contain the whole?

(I, 23)

With what imperturbable and untroubled ease, comparable to that of Shakespeare's 'cloud-capp'd towers', the couplets roll out their

[1] *Horace, Ep.* II, i, 281.
[2] See Warburton's note to I, 16.

mighty images. So the poet asks why man complains. Weak though he be, why expect to be strong? Just as the lamb is ignorant of human purpose, so is man of the divine. The lamb 'licks the hand just rais'd to shed his blood', a merciful Providence blinding it: Pope's sympathy with small animals is again noteworthy. But, small or large, it is the same to God, whom we are shown in a great passage intent on His purposes, seeing 'with equal eye' either 'a hero perish or a sparrow fall', atoms or whole systems destroyed, 'and now a bubble burst and now a world' (I, 35–90). The smooth and controlled statement here lifts the mind to that final serenity conditioning tragic art. Death will answer questions. Meanwhile a life-force beats in us with resurgent hope, and to that we must trust (I, 95). Pope's vitalistic philosophy is at once vast and simple, working from the patent fact that the race does not commit suicide. It aims at interpreting life itself.

As before, the hindrance to cosmic receptivity is 'reasoning pride', pride working through reason. Thus order is disturbed: 'Rejudge his justice, be the God of God.' Man would invert the universal laws. In pride he assumes the world was created for him alone, that nature's riches are all for him. Yes, but what of nature's cruelty? Of earthquakes and tempests? Are not these natural as a spring morning? If so, why should not human evil, that of a Borgia or a Catiline, form needed part of the one great design? Notice (i) the reference of human evil to earthquakes and tempests, as in the Shakespearian symbolism; and (ii) the preliminary forgiveness of all evil which we may suppose to be at the back of Shakespeare's work. Sound reason, says Pope, must 'submit'; and indeed Jesus' doctrine of God's non-human justice was very similar. To Pope, conflicts are necessary. The great 'all' is based on elemental strife, and 'passions' are the *élan vital* of existence: the Shakespearian analogy is again obvious, passionate conflict being the very hub and axle of Shakespearian drama. All this, whatever, if any, its limitations, is a philosophy integral to tragic art. Moreover, though these disquietudes occur, the 'general order' in nature and man, the stability of the whole, is not in danger, as in *Richard II*, *Julius Caesar*, *Hamlet*, *Macbeth*, where order is felt as ultimately and inevitably undisturbed (I, 113–72).

The nice balance of human and animal faculties is analysed. Do we envy the fly's 'microscopic eye'? Given a more delicate sense-perception, who knows but that we might 'die of a rose in aromatic pain'? Were our hearing keener, tuned to a different wave-length, we might be stunned by the thunders of the cosmic music. Each life-form has its gifts, the lynx its sight, the hound his keen scent (I, 193–214). Great nature beats in the poetry, its vast and tiny miracles inspiring equal awe:

The spider's touch, how exquisitely fine!
Feels at each thread, and lives along the line.

(I, 217)

Man's sense-perception and thought are subtly balanced with thin division. In this vast mystery of air, ocean, earth, all alive and pregnant with creative energies—'all matter quick and bursting into birth'—this *living* universe, where life is graded step by step upward, magnificently ordered into an 'amazing whole', where one disruption might upset all, why should man complain? Pope senses those same creative forces that so tingle in Goethe's *Faust*, however they be levelled under his own smoother harmonies. Would you have angels and suns, he asks, reorganized for your needs? That were at once madness, pride and impiety. It is as though the 'foot' or 'hand' should rebel against the head; the thought is continually of nature and organic life (I, 233–60). The 'great creating nature' of *The Winter's Tale* is Pope's explicit theme.

Pope attacks man's self-confident *reason*. It was, earlier, his violent aversion:

In Pride, in reas'ning Pride, our error lies;
All quit their sphere, and rush into the skies.
Pride still is aiming at the blest abodes,
Men would be Angels, Angels would be Gods.

(I, 123)

Which may be read as an unintended criticism of Milton, whose nature is so continually humanized, eternalized, and in whom human impulse is all but petrified through a too tyrannic 'reason'.[1] The truer wisdom is piety towards God, or Nature. For

All are but parts of one stupendous whole,
Whose body Nature is and God the soul.

(I, 267)

[1] For Milton's own *use* of the concept, see my note on p. 174 below.

An inexhaustible and magical life-force 'operates' ubiquitous and eternally 'unspent':

> *As full, as perfect, in a hair as heart:*
> *As full, as perfect, in vile Man that mourns,*
> *As the rapt Seraph that adores and burns.*
>
> (I, 276)

The natural and the divine are not in conflict; there is a graded ascent, but no opposition. Therefore:

> *Submit—In this, or any other sphere,*
> *Secure to be as blest as thou canst bear:*
> *Safe in the hand of one disposing Pow'r,*
> *Or in the natal, or the mortal hour.*
> *All Nature is but Art, unknown to thee;*
> *All Chance, Direction which thou can'st not see;*
> *All Discord, Harmony not understood;*
> *All partial Evil, universal Good:*
> *And, spite of Pride, in erring Reason's spite,*
> *One truth is clear, Whatever is, is right.*
>
> (I, 285)

See how the thought moves in terms vast and unethical corresponding to the symbolisms rooted in Shakespearian drama. This trust, lucid and impregnable in its cosmic grip, is necessary alike to any poetic or religious conception of the whole. It may be related in particular to the New Testament, Shakespeare, and Shelley's *Defence of Poetry*.[1] Such pre-eminently positive and vitalistic works might today be grouped together to form the basis of a new classicism, at once naturalistic and religious: that is, a body of doctrine which can be accepted, normally, by every educated person. There are few safer guides to such a faith than Pope, since he is never submerged by his own ocean-roll of rhythm, as Milton, nor burned by his own fire, as Shelley. He offers what is perhaps the most valuable of all insights: a coherent romanticism. This is reached through (i) a sense of ever-springing life in nature, the continual miracle of existence, and (ii) a dominating sense of the cosmic whole. Each, of course,

[1] The comparison of Pope's lines and Shelley's *Defence of Poetry* has since been developed in *Christ and Nietzsche* (1948), I, 20; III, 104. For Shelley, see also V, 175, note; 179; 201–2.

involves the other. The doctrine is positive, not negative; interpretative, not critical; got by a humility washing the mind transparent to see what is before its eyes. It is the conditioning starting-point for all wisdom.

Why, then, does it fail to satisfy? Only because a static philosophy, as such, must; must in fact contradict itself. For if all is perfect, why complain of man's absurd pride? Why write any poem at all, since all action implies dissatisfaction? Yet Jesus' philosophy of love fails before the Pharisees who raise his wrath: there is always a good and evil while man remains an active force. Universal acceptance will never lead to an ultimate placidity in, at all events, a western mind; and observe that the discrepancy involves the problem of *action*. And yet this very discrepancy points us back to a provisional solution, for the final test is not static either. We should not ask 'Is the world as I see it perfect?' but rather, 'Does the belief in a final harmony *in practice* lead me to action that proves, however illogically, creative?' The problem centres finally on this question of subjective experience, and it will be seen how Pope in his second Epistle takes more precisely into account the dynamic of the human mind or soul. That is not, however, his business here.

As a statement of a positive acceptance conditioning creative action, the *Essay on Man* and Jesus' central assurance God = Love remain impregnable, and likewise appear to condition any satisfactory creations of epic or dramatic force in poetry. But, again, it is one thing to know God's love when you read a ghastly news-story in the morning paper, and quite another to feel the same when such a shadow creeps near your own life: trust in the universal harmony, though it may readily be known, is rarely to be lived through to the end. The best philosophic poetry, even the creative psychology which we shall study in Pope's second Epistle, leaves a want: if it did not, there would be no need for the New Testament drama, as complementary to its doctrine, Shakespeare's plays, or *Eloisa to Abelard*. These hold an extra dimension of shared action and shared experience: we are made to feel, however weakly, the hero's agony, whilst at the same instant knowing, however confusedly, the more inclusive harmony. The sharing is now part of our acceptance; dramatic, not philosophic, with an emotional validity beyond static theory. Hence *Paradise Lost* must be considered a far greater work than Pope's *Essay*, since, even though Milton be wrong and Pope right on the most crucial of poetic issues, Milton's Satan remains of more worth than any philosophy.[1] This is, fundamentally, the cause of the disparity between Jesus' simple doctrine and the complexities of Christian ritual and dogma, and it perhaps follows that the Christian Church errs in opposing pantheism rather than working for an inclusive assertion. Pope's first Epistle remains, like Jesus' faith, as true as any such philosophic statement can be: though itself static, it takes fully into account the dynamic of life, stressing the upsurging forces of nature continually, and specifically including evils. As a static philosophy, it will never be superseded while the human race is here to philosophize; but such philosophy, as we know it, may, and indeed must, be complemented by a more dynamic, subjective thinking such as Pope moves to in his second Epistle; which will depend also on our understanding of the New Testament drama, religious ritual generally, and especially tragic literature. Milton flies, like a moth to a flame, and with something of the same noble and selfless perversity, into the very centre of this problem, always working from the disharmony between nature and God, and caught in the spidery web of the problems involved by human free will and action. He is in *Paradise Lost* too much involved in his own fiction; Pope in the *Essay on Man*, if only because it is an essay and not a drama, too little; blend the two and you get Shakespearian tragedy, Milton's own Satan, or *Eloisa to Abelard*.[2]

Pope once finely approaches the mystery in his Essay:

So Man, who here seems principal alone,
Perhaps acts second to some sphere unknown,
Touches some wheel, or verges to some goal;
'Tis but a part we see, and not a whole.

(I, 57)

This darkly shadows a most important truth, the exploration of which is the central purpose of all my interpretations, for this sense

[1] The thought here is intricate, but its validity has since been supported by Maynard Mack who follows my argument in using a similar contrast of Pope's statement with Milton's Satan in point of 'dramatic' depth, his word 'ceremonial' balancing my use of 'ritual' below (*Twickenham* edition, Int., lxxiii).

[2] The central problem discussed in this paragraph has since been neatly handled by R. J. Z. Werblowsky, in *Lucifer and Prometheus* (1952). He argues that the acceptance of evil must always be limited to the past, and that in any 'concrete situation' involving choice such an acceptance must, failing some 'radical psychological revision of the values of good and evil', remain inapplicable (VI, 100).

of some new dimension beyond direct knowledge exactly corresponds to the shared, lived, mystery of tragic ritual, whether religious or artistic. See how a geometrical and mechanical symbol, so unusual in Pope, assists for once this deliberate penetration. Such a penetration is often reflected in literature into some cogent, often supernatural, symbolism thrown up by the dramatic conflict, and yet also the very heart of the work concerned: the voice of eternity in the 'sainted maid', together with earlier similar impressions, is such an integrating and resolving symbol in *Eloisa to Abelard*. Throughout the *Essay on Man* there is an explicit belief in extra dimensions of existence beyond the sensible-human, of angelic hierarchies and purposes. They are, unlike Milton's divine beings, left undefined, and this lack corresponds precisely to that sense of a great otherness so often given negative definition by tragic art. We could say that all art works as much through what it leaves unsaid as through what it says, and hence the positive force so mysteriously inhering in the baffling technique of reserve generally which Pope so finely masters. Our four lines accordingly express the fundamental meaning of tragic art: the revelation, through experience, of some purpose, beyond the individual, fulfilled by suffering.

In Epistle II Pope concentrates on man. He attacks science, contrasting its supposed certitudes concerning the majestic and mysterious universe with man's hopeless ignorance of, and lack of mastery over, himself. It then concentrates on the instinct of self-love as the primary thrust of human nature. Reason, we are told, can look ahead and guide, but is not the motor force. Pope sternly reproves thinkers who regard instinct and reason as enemies: 'More studious to divide than to unite', they are happiest when 'at war about a name'; and we may say the same about certain critical concepts that have since helped to fog the naturalistic synthesis of Pope's own *Essay*. So Pope's attack is levelled against reason *in isolation*, when out of touch with the creative principle (II, 1–92). When he rejects a virtuous stoicism 'fix'd as in a frost', we may be reminded of Milton's motionless and resisting Lady in *Comus*, and Jesus in *Paradise Regained*. In a passage closely following a speech of Nestor in *Troilus and Cressida* we are shown the grandeur of 'exercise' under spiritual 'tempest', when God himself 'mounts the storm, and walks upon the wind'. All passions can be directed for good, they are indeed the necessary gale to drive on the ship; various emotions may be harmoniously blended; man cannot, we are told, destroy what he is himself composed of. We are urged towards a light-and-shade harmony tuned, with reason's help, to natural and divine purpose.

There follows a piercing analysis of dangerous 'master passions', explaining how they draw to them all natural forces of the personality with deadly success, and how, mothered by 'nature' and nursed by 'habit', they grow stronger by the help of other faculties. Evil is here deliberately related to nature; but Pope's ordering and directing of the psychological drama are very different from Milton's. He repudiates mental for more vital categories: 'rules' are no help where 'arms' are needed; to 'mourn' is not to 'mend'; reason (here = conscience) may be 'a sharp accuser but a helpless friend'. He suggests that such thinking may prove deceptive, and insidiously make matters worse, as may seem to happen with Milton and Marlowe, whose poetry can be far more dangerously sensuous than Shakespeare's or Pope's, as though they are simultaneously condemning and enjoying (II, 101–60). Pope's way is eminently practical. Nature's road 'must ever be preferred'. Reason by itself is here not even a 'guide', of no *positive* help, but it may well be of negative use, and 'guard' against disaster:

> *'Tis hers to rectify, not overthrow,*
> *And treat this passion more as friend than foe.*
>
> (II, 163)

We have a psychology of integration that fits Shakespearian tragedy, and the sense we receive that the energy there displayed, as Keats once said in another context, remains, in essence, fine. It also ranges itself with Pope's holistic arguments elsewhere. We begin to see how, through the medium of a personal psychology, Pope has gone far to blend a universal acceptance with moral categories. He does not repudiate his first Epistle, but shows how, even though 'nature' may originate evils, the trust in her harmony may remain *creatively true*; and he next outlines examples of dangerous passions proving creative if well used. A virtue rooted in instinct, almost, one might say, in vice, grows strong, body and mind acting as one whole, 'wild Nature's vigor working at the root', the fine naturalistic emphasis recalling certain of Jesus' parables. Lust, we are told, may become love, sloth turn into philosophical meditation, while thought of what vices lie at the root even of our virtues may serve as a salutary check to pride. As for any more immediate and practical distinctions of good from evil, they are left, and perhaps must be, to 'the God within the mind'; probably a more secure trust than modern scepticism would allow. It is admitted that vice, as vice, can be real and increase through habit, though it should, normally, be instinctively hated and therefore, we may suppose, transmuted, in so far as seen and understood; the implication being that virtue is fundamentally the more instinctive. Yet we are told to remember always that virtue and vice are both parts of the self, and each self part of a greater whole, with which Heaven is mainly concerned, using different personalities for different, subsidiary, purposes, and building from defects the glory of creation (II, 175–248). The thought reflects the Shakespearian integrity while helping to define the Miltonic indecision. In Epistle II *the good-and-evil antinomy is all but resolved through a dynamic psychology serving as a transition from total acceptance to ethical discrimination.*[1]

So the third Epistle widens again from the individual to society, itself part of a cosmic drama felt as *positive activity*, wherein atoms cohere, matter blends with matter, dying vegetation produces new life, and all perishing forms are aspects of one vast vitality like bubbles on water: 'by turns we catch the vital breath, and die'. All parts blend into a single whole, one 'soul' connecting and preserving all, nothing, and the rule is observed by Pope's own poetic phrases, existing for itself alone. Man must not centralize nature in himself, as Milton's imagery tends to do, the bird does not sing primarily for him, the horse enjoys the ride. However, man alone attains unselfishness and imaginative power: the jay cannot admire the 'insect's gilded wings'. Animals preserved for slaughter have a good time first and do not foresee the doom man ultimately shares with them; and, by a similar prevision of nature, death never *seems* near to man. Notice the illumination of a simple but vast human truth through a natural analogy (III, 1–78).

There is again an emphasis on the respect due to instinct. Reason —we should say 'intelligence'—is generally slow to serve, but 'honest Instinct comes a volunteer', and, moreover, invariably hits its mark: the contrast is that between intuitive genius and laboured skill in any activity whatsoever, in life, art, or play. Instinct is 'quick' and tireless, reason 'heavier', and soon weary. Instinct makes for action; reason

[1] This, the core of my interpretation, has been accepted, with acknowledgment, by Maynard Mack as the core of his own: 'One of the functions of this epistle is to effect a transition from a mood of theodicy ("submit") to a mood of ethics' (*Twickenham* edition, lxi).

is merely a 'comparing' power. The one is permanent and 'must go right', whereas the other is intermittent and 'may go wrong' (III, 79–96). So

> *... Reason raise o'er Instinct as you can,*
> *In this 'tis God directs, in that 'tis Man.*
>
> (III, 97)

'This' means, of course, 'instinct' in Pope's latinized syntax. The argument is part of a general tradition, or development, from the New Testament to Blake and Nietzsche. Nor is it quite so mad as it sounds: Keats likewise urged the sanctity of the heart's instinct. Nature that made the 'spider' design his 'parallels' (III, 103) can look after men. Pope, unlike Shakespeare and Swift, seems to have a warm corner in his heart for spiders. In this, as in much else, he is with Byron.

God, in designing the great whole, plants various bounds to the nature of all beings, whose bliss depends on mutual help. Union is really an instinctive end, since one nature feeds the vital flame of all creation:

> *Whate'er of life all-quick'ning aether keeps,*
> *Or breathes thro' air, or shoots beneath the deeps,*
> *Or pours profuse on earth, one nature feeds*
> *The vital flame, and swells the genial seeds.*
>
> (III, 115)

In the 'fierce embrace' of sexual love nature's essential harmony is realized. This expands to love of children and, with reason's help, farther. Men know 'habitual' as well as 'natural' love: that is, lasting and deep emotions. From these charity is born. This use of parental love as a transition from the sexual-erotic to what St. Paul called 'agapé' is most important, but the use of 'habitual' is also neat, since the deeper love may often develop through habit alone (III, 119–46).

Nature's absolute rule was God's rule, and at first all was peace. But, since then, man has fallen to blood-sacrifice, slaughtered beasts for food, and become an enemy to himself (III, 147–68).[1] Pope does not reconcile this directly with his former optimism and the many obvious cruelties within nature. Man's slaughter of animals has from

[1] In his valuable study *The Golden Feast* (1952), Mr. Roy Walker has collected a wealth of material from mythology and poetry supporting the vegetarian philosophy. Pope is writing in this tradition.

the start troubled him, and may seem to dislocate the precision of his *Essay* considered as a whole. But he has been steadily making a most difficult transition from general acceptance to moral distinctions. We have already suggested that no static conception can do this, and we must not contrast Epistle III with Epistle I without remembering Epistle II. Until the very complex implications of this process are fully grasped, the separate Epistles are perhaps best read as independent approaches to the mysteries of human life: the first philosophical, the second mainly psychological, the third ethical. 'Nature' is throughout a binding and fusing concept, and the whole poem may be, provisionally, allowed to enjoy an artistic rather than a purely logical coherence. Yet perhaps nowhere in literature can we so clearly see, by regarding the place of Epistle II in the sequence, how there is logic of the most subtle and profound sort within the *arrangement* of any true artistic whole. We are watching something very rare: a poetic genius of the first order deliberately setting himself in maturity to create a compact and coherent system from his own creative centre.

Pope next describes man's progress to civilization, how human art copies birds, ants, and bees, the close reference of human and natural communities reminding us of *Henry V*. Nature, with finer laws than man, knows 'anarchy without confusion', a phrase throwing back to *Windsor Forest*; and this cannot be improved on by reason, which only entangles 'justice' in 'law' (III, 169–98). So societies and kings come into being. At first the patriarch was 'king, priest, and parent' in one, and led to the worship of a single father-God. All was well before 'wit oblique' scattered the 'steady light'. Disasters follow: tyrants, conquests, superstitions, devils. Pride and force come into play; emotional directions go crooked, 'fear' makes 'devils', and 'weak hope' constitutes religious faith. The divine is now felt as 'partial, changeful, passionate, unjust', gods are made in the likeness of 'tyrants', 'pride' builds a heaven and 'spite' a hell. Some of this fits pre-Christian theologies, but if we remember Milton's excessive and barbaric royalisms, Pope may be felt closer to his own day whenever he refers to force, or when he sees 'zeal' rather than 'charity' at the helm of religion (III, 199–262). Now all naturalistic faith is quickly lost:

Then sacred seem'd th' ethereal Vault no more.

(III, 263)

Remember how the elements of nature are in *Paradise Regained* (II, 121–6) under demonic domination. Pope, like Milton, believes in a 'fall', but there is a vast difference. His centre of judgement is never the fallen consciousness, which cannot prescribe to man's sinful state any more than the blind can lead the blind. Rather he is to be ranged with Keats in his emphasis on a past naturalistic piety; with Byron in his horror of blood-sacrifice; and with Shelley in his hatred of theological tyrannies. Milton, of course, has similar 'romantic' directions, and probably later poets owe him more than they think, but his poetic faith is disrupted by the attempt to force together incompatible systems.

To continue. That self-love driving man to crime makes him also protect himself against it: 'all join to guard what each desires to gain'. The bad logic and the suicidal quality of selfishness are excellently shown. Any great 'follower of God', 'poet' or 'patriot', aims only to rekindle nature's ancient light, to restore mankind as a whole to its fundamental instinct, the doctrine of both Jesus and Shelley. All Pope's thought is based on such vast natural directions: so, though different forms of government and religion arise in turn, that man 'can't be wrong whose life is in the right'. Truth is felt as a vital direction, not a mental concept or any arrangement of concepts, and the resolution of the *Essay's* central paradox is again implicit. So charity, which involves action, is greater than faith or hope, being 'all mankind's concern', inevitably and instinctively, however little they know or like it. Man, 'like the vine', can only gain strength from an 'embrace', self-love and social love being, at the last, identical (III, 269–312). The argument has a beautiful simplicity and precision, and may be profitably related today to our economic and international problems. One passage (III, 289–302) on order recalls Ulysses' order-speech in *Troilus and Cressida*.

The *Essay's* four parts are alternately general and personal, and the last Epistle treats of happiness:

> *That something still which prompts th' eternal sigh,*
> *For which we bear to live, or dare to die,*
> *Which still so near us, yet beyond us lies . . .*
>
> (IV, 3)

The touch is wistful, humble, and deeply understanding. Pope brings a Shakespearian insight to this simple yet vast issue, on which the 'learned' are consistently 'blind', taking extreme positions, either trusting in 'everything' or utterly agnostic (IV, 19–26); nor should a proper sympathy with Pope's whole argument accuse his own *Essay* of the facile trust indicated, since it shirks no tragedies of mortal existence, nor any moral evils, but rather sees into and through them. Behind the isolated selfishness of robber, tyrant, hermit, or proclaimed hater of man, he sees a lurking love, a desire for admiration or friendship. One common longing is felt behind all humanity. Happiness is not a matter of material circumstance, which indeed tends to negate itself, since wealth of any sort leads to fear and lack of it may condition hope. But the final peace rests in simplicity and virtue: 'And Peace, oh Virtue! Peace is all thy own.' Virtue naturally meets man's approval (IV, 39–88). The statement bears to the acceptance of moral evil in the first Epistle precisely the somewhat obscure relation borne by Macbeth's, or Richard III's, necessary condemnation within the play to the equally important artistic delight the spectator derives from his crime, Pope's thinking all along running parallel to the issues raised by study of Shakespeare, or any great tragic artist. We are reminded that noble self-sacrifice proves rather a willing 'contempt of life' than the inefficiency of virtue (IV, 102). God is next cleared, not altogether satisfactorily, of responsibility for certain evils in terms of general law, in that He does not abrogate the law of gravitation to prevent a death, the thought again involving the concept of the whole (IV, 111–30). There follows an incisive argument on simple virtue's essential independence of outward suffering or rewards, giving instead 'the soul's calm sunshine, and the heart-felt joy' (IV, 168). It is acutely observed that fame is really a matter of one's own circle, since the rest does not touch you (IV, 239). A striking autobiographical paragraph asserts that superior gifts bring only trouble: 'All fear, none aid you, and few understand' (IV, 266). An expanded contrast of simple integrity with the shams of worldly place and power follows Wolsey's advice in *Henry VIII*, and points towards Pope's own doctrine in the *Satires* (IV, 269–326). The way to happiness is through identity with the vast chain of being and rising whole that is the *Essay's* main argument. Our very aspirations are evidence of something beyond, since nature does not implant meaningless faculties; as so often, the thought is flashingly new. We are last brought to a vision of widening circles of altruism and a reiteration of the claim implied in nearly every line of the poem to have held up 'Nature's light' instead of 'Wit's false mirror' (IV, 327–

372; 393). 'Wit' in Pope is variously used: here it means 'human reason', normally something like 'intellectual talent', sometimes even 'poetic genius'.[1] It is here felt as specifically academic, perhaps contemporary: Pope's thought is probably dwelling on writers of his own day.

Pope's mature theory on man and his universe relates exactly to his *Essay on Criticism*, his own poetic practice, and his satires: to his nature-feeling, sympathetic human warmth, and sense of the artistic whole. His *Essay* is far from easy, but much of its difficulty is removed once it can be felt as a dynamic rather than a purely static statement. He works to substitute vital directions and a living psychology for dead concepts, with a strong sense of the marsh-like insecurity of rigid terms, as in his suggestion that the ethical reason alone may surreptitiously pander to the very vice it condemns (II, 155–60); or when he considers arguments concerning the 'forms of government' mere folly whilst putting emphasis instead on the *way* those forms are administered (III, 303). He keeps his eye steadily on the final test of action, individual or communal. The cosmic trust throughout may be related both to Bacon's *Advancement of Learning* and to Shelley's *Defence of Poetry*, and clearly touches certain modern tendencies with which it has not been as yet associated; as, for example, the naturalism of Henri Bergson; the holism of Jan Smuts, whose remarkable book *Holism and Evolution* adds a valuable concept to our vocabulary; and the all but excessive vitalism of Lawrence's *Fantasia of the Unconscious*. This only those, to use Pope's phrase, 'more studious to divide than to unite' (p. 49), can fail to recognize. Such rigid divisions are, it would seem, rooted in an unconscious fear that wills the dispersal of positive forces in order to avoid their massed significance.[2]

IV

The Dunciad (1728; final version, 1743) stands apart from both the *Essay on Man* and the satiric epistles. In handling with a poetic sublimity those personalities of the book-world whom he most despises, the poet fuses extremes to give us a mock-heroic of the

[1] Pope's use of 'wit' has now been discussed by William Empson in *The Structure of Complex Words* (1952).

[2] Additional remarks on the *Essay on Man* are offered on pp. 169–82 below. For its relation to 'religion' as normally understood, see especially p. 178.

same genre as *The Rape of the Lock*, but with a diametrically opposite tone. It is Pope's attempt to fit his worst particular experiences into the harmonies of great art after the universal principle symbolized by Dante's final vision of the divine circle mysteriously fitted to and enclosing, though how the poet cannot say, the human form. The resolving medium is humour as rich in its way as that of *The Rape of the Lock*. The particular references, on understanding of which the humour must partly depend, are unfortunately somewhat tedious, though they give rise to some entertaining notes by the author. That the subject should be so personal may seem regrettable, but the peculiar nature of the poem may be supposed to define the conditions under which alone a work of narrative, and even more one of heroic, art was felt by the poet to be possible. As in Dante, the poet's own negative experiences force themselves shamelessly forward; but, while personal records are certainly involved, general experiences, and not persons, are really in question, though the poet himself cannot quite be expected to know this. Literature was at this period the medium through which an old culture was felt to be in transit to a new, and the nature of its contemporary practitioners was intuitively recognized as a matter of vital national, if not racial, concern. *The Dunciad* objectifies the genius of its age and is an artistic document of considerable importance.

The irritating preponderance of forgotten names is, as one of the notes all but suggests, itself part of the design, the persons seeming the more boring and therefore fatuous for our ignorance. The prevailing darkness of the poetic atmosphere is thereby increased, since you are forced to wade through a stifling, clinging, muddy, bog-like substance of intractable references. The poem has also actual bogs, mud, and even 'mud-nymphs' (II, 332). It is couched in Pope's more sensuous, rich-throated, slow manner, and loaded with naturalistic and biological reference. Pope's work never shows the Miltonic emphasis on the hard or metallic: 'brazen brightness' and 'polished hardness' are terms of exact critical opprobrium (I, 219–20), while his own impressions are naturalistic. The atmosphere is thick and heavy with fogs, clouds, 'rolling smoke' (I, 248), 'vapours blue' (III, 3), and, generally, palling darkness; a 'veil of fogs dilates' the awful face of the Goddess of Dulness (I, 262); people move in a 'black troop' (II, 360); the darkly-vowelled name 'Mundungus' (I, 234) sets the tone. Many small or supposedly dull-witted animals are used with the normal derogatory associations, as in the second book of *Gulliver's Travels*: such are donkeys, apes, puppies, owls, crabs, bugs, maggots. A strongly physical impact is usual, as in the exquisite

> *Round him much Embryo, much Abortion, lay,*
> *Much future Ode, and abdicated Play.*
>
> (I, 121)

The animals may, when more fully realized, both help the poem and yet show Pope's own natural sympathy, as in

> *So watchful Bruin forms, with plastic care,*
> *Each growing lump, and brings it to a Bear.*
>
> (I, 101)

Or in the picture of 'huge Lintot' running:

> *As when a dab-chick waddles through the copse*
> *On feet and wings, and flies, and wades, and hops.*
>
> (II, 63)

The cramming of jerky monosyllables into one line is a usual trick in Pope where absurdity is to be indicated, and the awkward motion implied may recall his own expressly athletic grace, sense of vital movement, and consummate ease: correspondingly he sees his opponents as dull, and heavy in motion. Mechanic imagery is a precise association for the dull and inorganic, and so bad poetry makes the muses 'scream like the winding of ten thousand jacks' (III, 160); dull, creaking, brains work strangely, like 'ponderous slugs' of lead (I, 182) pumped into motion by an air-gun, or clocks that go by the movement of a weight beneath (I, 183–4); the hero's head, guided by the Goddess, is as a bowl that goes 'obliquely waddling to the mark in view' (I, 172); Dulness 'lumbers' like a 'rolling stone' (III, 293–4). The joy lies in translating to clear physical terms the cumbersome inefficiencies of so abstract an art as literature: Pope makes the ordinary man realize how a bad artist appears to himself, and the humour is often richly satisfying. All movement is slow, as when old Dulness 'heaved the head' (I, 257); the world of *The Dunciad* is ludicrously harmonious and organic, being all stupid, dull, sleepy, with its sleepy 'poppy' (III, 317), 'sacred opium' (I, 288) and 'drunken vine' (I, 303). The Dunces start their ludicrous harmonies, like asses braying:

So swells each wind-pipe; Ass intones to Ass;
Harmonic twang! of leather, horn, and brass.

(II, 253)

Subtle nasality and inanimacy ('brass') are used by a poet of warm natural affinities to convey his impression of a dead art. But the impression may be more naturalistic, as when

Keen, hollow winds howl thro' the bleak recess

(I, 35)

to signify music caused by emptiness. The poetry relies throughout on heavy sensuous appeal, as when, again, the authors drive their audience to sleep:

Then mount the Clerks, and in one lazy tone
Thro' the long, heavy, painful page drawl on;
Soft creeping, words on words, the sense compose;
At ev'ry line they stretch, they yawn, they doze.

(II, 387)

Which we must read very, very slowly, giving the vowels and 'z' sounds their full chance. *The Dunciad* is the condemnation, by as vital a poet as any in our literature, of the insidiously academic writer, the poet of outward form lacking spiritual energy, in short, the charlatan; one who, because he is out of contact with the springs of life, is necessarily dull.

Heroic action is strongly physical; indeed, you may feel, too much so, when we come to Curll's misfortune in the race, his prayer to Jove, and subsequent recovery of speed 'renew'd by ordure's sympathetic force' (II, 103), and his later engaging in competition with 'salient spout' (II, 162) for a well-known authoress 'with cow-like udders and with ox-like eyes' (II, 164). The booksellers' competition is not for the squeamish. Sensibilities may well be offended, even when we rule out all consciousness of contemporary and personal reference; and yet the references are often such as, being fictional physical impressions of an inward reality, ought not to hurt more than direct reference to the vice intended, which is normally both dangerous and respectable. Pope gives full reasons in his notes, and we must suppose him sincere. Where there is a true humour, the physical images perform a cathartic purpose of the most general kind. The mud-diving competition, with the exquisite 'mud-nymphs', is surely most happily conceived to objectify the muck-raking of slanderous authors, and attains a mock solemnity that is too deeply humorous to be finally cruel:

> *When lo! a burst of thunder shook the flood;*
> *Slow rose a form, in majesty of Mud;*
> *Shaking the horrors of his sable brows,*
> *And each ferocious feature grim with ooze.*
>
> (II, 325)

To be read with a reverential and measured sonority. The humour depends on a discrepancy between true dignity and Pope's long-standing *bête noire* of unjustifiable and ludicrous pride. It can scarcely have done these heavy gentlemen harm for once to see themselves sinking 'with all the might of gravitation blest' (II, 318). A fine Miltonic transposition shows us one of them waiting his turn at the dive:

> *In naked majesty Oldmixon stands . . .*
>
> (II, 283)

What soft cohesive grandeur in the stately utterance! The image remains a noble warning to the human race.

The epic's beginning sets the note of gravity and bathos in happy balance:

> *The Mighty Mother, and her Son, who brings*
> *The Smithfield Muses to the ear of Kings,*
> *I sing.*
>
> (I, 1)

Book II starts with a Miltonic parody. But the essence of grandeur is quite purely transmitted: it is real, though its application be mockery. Just as the Goddess' temple has its 'sacred Dome' (I, 265), so the poetry has its own sanctity and shadowed grace, often with a mighty voice softened to nature's splendours:

> *. . . in yonder cloud behold,*
> *Whose sars'net skirts are edg'd with flamy gold,*
> *A matchless youth! his nod these worlds controls,*
> *Wings the red lightning, and the thunder rolls.*
>
> (III, 253)

Which seems almost wasted in a passage which is, as a whole, a magnificent exposure of absurd stage elaborations that make 'a new world to Nature's laws unknown' (III, 241). As in *The Rape of the Lock*, ritualistic dignity is used, though with a greater satiric intention. So we watch our hero setting the flames to his sacrifice of unsuccessful plays:

> *And thrice he lifted high the Birth-day brand,*
> *And thrice he dropt it from his quiv'ring hand;*
> *Then lights the structure, with averted eyes:*
> *The rolling smoke involves the sacrifice.*
> *The op'ning clouds disclose each work by turns. . . .*
>
> (I, 245)

The first two lines are a parody on epic narrative that may remind us that the satire is throughout two-edged: there is a criticism of vacuous sublimity as well as criticism of trivial substance. But we can also feel, in these—to borrow Keats' phrase—'huge cloudy symbols' of an absurd pomp, these domes, temples, and altars, or the 'rev'rend flamen' of II, 354, a rich, Keatsian, apprehension of the sacred.[1]

The whole work has, to quote Flecker's *Hassan*, a 'monstrous beauty like the hindquarters of an elephant'.[2] It moves with a similar cumbersome ease. The imaginative consistency recalls Dante's *Inferno*, which it resembles far more closely than Milton's Hell. Like Dante's poem, it is, to quote this time from *The Testament of Beauty* (III, 244), cluttered with 'earthly tangle', though whether it lie equally near to the 'throne of God' will perhaps be questioned. It has at least one claim to lie nearer, since there is a strange and happy absence of the sadistic.[3] The comedy is not precisely cruel: the dunces are all happy, are not shown as realizing their absurdity, and are allowed to maintain a certain physical, though ludicrous, dignity. Pope respects the physical to this extent, whereas he is merciless

[1] I have emphasized the sensuous qualities in Pope's poetry. Both J. Middleton Murry, in his essay 'The Poetry of William Collins' (*Countries of the Mind*, First Series, 1931), and F. R. Leavis, in *Revaluation* (1936), have stressed a relationship to the Metaphysicals. See also Maynard Mack's contribution to *Pope and his Contemporaries*, ed. J. L. Clifford and L. A. Landa (Oxford, 1949). Dr. Leavis' argument has been opposed by F. W. Bateson in *English Poetry* (1950; XIV, 254).

[2] Edith Sitwell, probably the first to appreciate this quality, has observed 'a kind of smoky and appalling beauty' permeating the poem (XVIII, 276).

[3] A penetration of the sadistic element in Dante's *Inferno* is one of the many profound insights of John Cowper Powys' *The Pleasures of Literature* (London, 1938; New York, under the title *The Enjoyment of Literature*, 1938).

when explicitly referring to ethical or artistic faults; and so Cibber, Oldmixon, and even Curll, have, in a sense, their own personal rights, like Sir Plume (p. 25). Dante's whippings and bodies stuck upside-down are, of course, part of a deadly serious statement, but Pope's delicate emotional and sensuous touch, felt in the softness, the nature-tone, of the whole atmosphere, is witnessed by his avoidance of what in his poem of mainly humorous intention would have been dangerous indeed. His few but somewhat callous references to poverty may be regarded as part of the metaphoric scheme in that they help to underline a mental and spiritual poverty. Shakespearian phrases often ring similarly callous with less excuse, offending a certain delicacy which has now become natural, whereas in the social consciousness of the past vagabondage and villainy had been identified. *The Dunciad* is Pope's *Inferno*, his *Macbeth*. That it refuses any violent evil is characteristic, for he writes from a mental horizon where such depths are not of primary importance: he feels, to adapt a phrase from Lyly's *Campaspe* (I, i, 82), 'letters' taking the place of 'lances'; and that is why his accusation of 'dulness' goes deeper than you might think, implying, as it does, a lack of mental vitality, and therefore of all those cosmic contacts on which the *Essay on Man* insists. Moreover, the poet's most intense personal antagonisms are next lifted as a weighty mallet to drive in his more general challenge, the whole mass of his emotional abhorrence in Books I to III—and they are mainly emotional and impressionistic, with slight attempt at rational analysis—being propelled in the subsequently added Book IV (1742) to establish a more philosophical charge, levelled at a whole culture.

In Book III the dunces are warned 'not to scorn your God' (III, 224). Book IV at once introduces us to abstract terms: Science in chains, Logic 'gagged and bound', Rhetorick stripped and languishing, Morality strangled, 'Mathesis' alone given freedom for her madness, but the Muses in 'ten-fold bonds' (IV, 21–36). The charge later emphasizes all the usual complaints, flattery in a 'sacred gown' (IV, 97), and, 'last and worst', that hypocrisy of the Muse, 'wit' without 'soul' (IV, 99–100). School education has become a meaningless discipline:

> *To ask, to guess, to know, as they commence,*
> *As Fancy opens the* quick *springs of Sense,*
> *We ply the* Memory, *we load the brain,*

> *Bind rebel Wit, and double* chain *on* chain;
> Confine *the thought, to exercise the breath;*
> *And keep them in the pale of* Words *till death.*
>
> (IV, 155)

I romanize crucial concepts. Universities come off no better. They dole out 'fragments, not a meal' (IV, 230). The 'critic Eye' acts as a 'microscope of Wit', studying 'hairs and pores', while quite missing how 'parts relate to parts or they to the whole', blind to 'the body's harmony, the beaming soul' (IV, 233–6). Something of the sort, surely, has happened with the study of Pope's own work, weighting him with labels. His own emphasis is still on the organic, the vitalistic, and set dead against all rigidities that would '*petrify* a Genius to a Dunce' (IV, 264; italics mine); against the 'cement' that binds together and reduces all mentalities to 'one dead level' (IV, 267–8). The stony and infertile are images of evil. The poetry, as before, is scattered with animal references, though these scarcely always maintain the precise animal tonings of Books I–III: to the silkworm (IV, 253), the adder (IV, 373), the fox (IV, 351), the humming-bird (IV, 446), with a delightful couplet on bees (IV, 79–80). There are exquisite descriptions of an exotic flower and a butterfly, which a scientist is satirized for having killed (IV, 403–36). We must not let Pope's or Swift's seeming over-stress of scientific indictment blind us to the substantial truth of their charges, at least where the humanities are concerned:

> *'Tis true, on Words is still our whole debate,*
> *Disputes of* Me *or* Te, *of* aut *or* at,
> *To sound or sink in* cano, *O or A,*
> *Or give up Cicero to C or K.*
>
> (IV, 219)

God is replaced by a mechanic causality, and concepts of 'matter' and 'space' (IV, 475–6), pride making man 'the final cause' of the universe (IV, 478). Scientists are ironically commanded to

> *See Nature in some partial narrow shape*
> *And let the Author of the Whole escape.*
>
> (IV, 455)

The proper *Dunciad* atmosphere is, on the whole, maintained, but the verse gets more taut and swift, as in the *Imitations of Horace*, and the book's more philosophic statement neatly links it with the *Essay on Man*: 'Be proud, be selfish, and be dull' (IV, 582).

We end with a prophecy of utter chaos, the heavy abstractions falling like the vast folds of a curtain to blot out the shows of human civilization:

> *Thus at her felt approach, and secret might,*
> Art *after* Art *goes out, and all is Night.*
> *See skulking* Truth *to her old cavern fled,*
> *Mountains of Casuistry heap'd o'er her head!*
> Philosophy, *that lean'd on Heav'n before,*
> *Shrinks to her second cause, and is no more.*
>
> (IV, 639)

All knowledge, losing contact with its true centre, turns 'giddy', turns in on itself, as today we have seen it do so clearly:

> *See* Mystery *to* Mathematics *fly!*
> *In vain! they gaze, turn giddy, rave and die.*
>
> (IV, 647)

The exact penetration into the chaotic and undisciplined, because unrooted, thought of the next two hundred years is almost uncanny. And now, since without the inner pulse of vital experience all sanctities are nothing,

> Religion *blushing veils her sacred fires,*
> *And unawares* Morality *expires.*
>
> (IV, 649)

'Chaos', the great 'anarch', rules. It is only too easy to shirk this challenge to our whole culture; to deny its precise relation to the warnings of Bacon's *Advancement of Learning*; and to Shelley's *Defence of Poetry*; to forget that respect for secondary causes still lingers deep in the twentieth-century mind, and that Pope's message stands above us, and beyond us, today.

V

From *The Rape of the Lock* and *Eloisa to Abelard* Pope moves, through *The Dunciad*, to philosophy and satire. Of these, the one is merely the obverse of the other, they are complementary, the *Essay on Man* being timeless and universal, and the satires particular and contemporary. This general move towards teaching, or prophecy, may be thought to register, in one sense, a fall, as Pope's compact line half-acknowledges, saying how, leaving 'Fancy's maze', he 'stoop'd to Truth and moraliz'd his song.'[1] But that is not the whole story. We watch poetry discarding heroic themes and aiming to achieve direct social impact; rather than describe actions, it becomes itself active. The pen was rapidly becoming a force comparable with the sword, and more is involved than literary jealousies or personal antagonisms. Besides, the nature of Pope's attack is of an importance reaching far beyond his own age. The *Essay on Man* presents a substantially new and vitalistic synthesis, which, though in spirit deriving from the New Testament, was nevertheless academically unorthodox and did not find another full poetic voice for half a century; and which is, moreover, of a positive power to meet with misunderstanding, resistance, and even hatred, in any age. Only in terms of this visionary positive can the satires receive a precise understanding.

Pope's negative position may be more closely defined, and is therefore more valuable, than Swift's.[2] Images of disgust are rather ethical than physical in their direction, resembling Shakespeare's, and the attack is strictly limited. Full-blooded crimes we have already seen equated with tempests and set among the harmonies of the *Essay*. These, being easily recognized, are of comparatively slight danger, and the attack concentrates on the more insidious and respectable vices, seen as some form of untruth to nature, loss of vital centres, insincerity, dishonesty, or pride. The conception is never rigid; we find rather an attempt at a very subtle, though often virulent, diagnosis. Society is shown as intrinsically self-contradictory, and individuals as lacking any wholeness of personality, any health.

We pass now to the *Moral Essays* (1731–5). In his *Epistle to Lord Cobham* [3] Pope attacks those who concentrate on second causes, and continues with a profound commentary on human nature. Personality, he says, cannot be reduced to reasoning and principles, any more than the dissecting of an animal can isolate its life for analysis. In personal relationships all is relevant to the observing subject, and

[1] *Epistle to Dr. Arbuthnot*, 341.

[2] See my essay 'Swift and the Symbolism of Irony', in *The Burning Oracle* (1939).

[3] *Moral Essays*, I.

we are very far from attaining to clarity concerning even our own motives (23–50). Men change from hour to hour, according to their employment, the time of day, the company they mix with, and reasoning can never bring down the elusive essences of such 'flying game' (63–98). All who argue from data and facts with 'retrospective eye', attempting to find the cause from inspection of the thing, the 'motive' from the 'deed', are on insecure ground (99–102). A good action need not originate from true goodness, nor does wise reasoning prove wisdom (109–18). We are urged to discover, presumably through intuition, a man's 'ruling passion', the centre of energy, when all should fall into perspective: otherwise you mistake 'the scaffold for the pile' (174–227). We may suggest that the discovery of certain centres of energy in Shakespeare and Pope serves similarly to clear up many confusions on the plane of conscious intention.[1]

Pope's emphasis on vital direction rather than any moral absolute or set of absolutes determines his human analysis. He sees wealth, as in the amazingly compact narrative of Sir Balaam,[2] doing the devil's work. His sense of the concretely vital is used to expose the appalling dangers inherent in the ever more abstract tendencies of finance, a hundred oxen being ironically imagined as arriving at a statesman's levee from a foreign country,[3] and the essential intangibility of the most dangerous vices being shown to work in double harness with the growing intangibility of wealth. Pope's positive emphasis is simple and concrete:

POPE: *What Riches give us let us then enquire:*
Meat, Fire, and Clothes.
BATHURST: *What more?*
POPE: *Meat, Clothes and Fire.*
(*Moral Essays*, III, 79)

In opposition, he paints the typical vulgarities of his age in *Moral Essays*, IV, with a description of a garden-design showing no 'art-ful wildness', each 'alley' symmetrically balanced by a 'brother', and 'trees cut to statues, statues thick as trees', the last line blending a reverence for natural life with a typical repudiation of mere artefacts (IV, 113–20). We are taken to a library well stocked with unread books, a lavatory where 'gaping Tritons spew to wash your face',

[1] Pope's arguments here may be aligned with what I have called the 'spatial' approach to literature or biography; see *Lord Byron: Christian Virtues* (1952), I, 47.
[2] *Moral Essays*, III, 339–402. [3] Ibid., III, 58.

and a dining-room of solemn grandeur more appropriate to a 'temple' or 'hecatomb' (IV, 133–56). It is all insincere and out of touch with the real situation, a forced hospitality:

> *In plenty starving, tantaliz'd in state,*
> *And complaisantly help'd to all I hate.*
>
> (IV, 163)

Against this we have a characteristic longing for golden corn again to 'embrown the slope', and wave above the forgotten ruins of a fallacious gaudiness (IV, 173–6).

The conception is Shakespearian: in *Timon of Athens* wealth and entertainment depend on living sincerities and, those gone, the palace crumbles; just as Enobarbus' allegiance to Antony's fortunes is conditioned by Cleopatra's faith. Pope's close kinship to Shakespeare is felt again in his *Epistle to a Lady*.[1] The feminine temperament is vividly and variously characterized: Atossa is an amazing study of dangerous vitality; Chloe is drawn from a violent reaction to the non-vital, recalling the Messenger's description of Octavia in *Antony and Cleopatra*; and a sympathetic treatment (269–80) of feminine complexity fits Cleopatra neatly. Pope senses a vital positive, and his view of women does not take the Miltonic turn, though he can be severe, as Byron seldom is. All Pope's most violently satirized people, even Chloe, are very much alive, though the most vivid are perhaps scarcely credible. Dryden in *Absalom and Achitophel* perhaps gains as a dramatist what he loses as a satirist, his Achitophel and Zimri being too well rounded, too composed, for the intended condemnation, at least for the kind of condemnation Pope brings to the creation of Sporus, his satiric portrait of Lord Hervey, in the *Epistle to Dr. Arbuthnot* (1735).

But Sporus is no mere personification of a thesis, nor even a type. He could not properly be fitted with a Jonsonian label:

POPE: *Let* Sporus *tremble—*
ARBUTHNOT: *What, that thing of silk,*
Sporus, *that mere white curd of Ass's milk?*
Satire or sense, alas! can Sporus *feel?*
Who breaks a butterfly upon a wheel?
POPE: *Yet let me flap this bug with gilded wings,*
This painted child of dirt, that stinks and stings;

[1] Ibid., II.

Whose buzz the witty and the fair annoys,
Yet wit ne'er tastes, and beauty ne'er enjoys. . . .

(305)

That he should be shown as not enjoying any full-blooded pleasures is necessary. Smiles show his emptiness 'as shallow streams run dimpling all the way'. He is created largely from vivid impressions of disgust, and is a 'toad half-froth, half-venom', who 'spits' himself abroad

In puns, or politics, or tales, or lies,
Or spite, or smut, or rhymes, or blasphemies.
His wit all see-saw, between that *and* this,
Now high, now low, now master up, now miss,
And he himself one vile Antithesis.

(321)

He is utterly insincere, a 'cherub' face disguising a serpent nature. The study has a striking and unforgettable vitality drawn from the poet's intense loathing, expressed first in jets of venom, then speeding into accumulations that whirl giddily, inducing sickness at an everlasting self-contradictory Nothingness. An utter lack of self-realization, of psychic wholeness, is indicated, together with a failure to fuse the masculine and feminine elements ('master' and 'miss' and, later, 'head' and 'heart') in the personality. 'Antithesis' sums the indictment, its strong force yet weak vowels reflecting a psychic discrepancy which has not attained the status of conflict: the subject is *content*, yet every instant offends against and denies Pope's philosophy of integration in the *Essay on Man*.[1] The use of monosyllabic jerks both makes for a puppet-like movement, though Sporus is more than a puppet, and acts as a fusillade of scorn; and what vitriol charges the exactly placed 'blasphemies'! Whatever or whoever the human prototype, or prototypes, this is scarcely a rounded study, but neither is there any single *idea* behind its creation, as there is, for example, behind Sir Epicure Mammon; rather is it caught straight from contact with those human personalities stated by Pope himself to be irreducible to concepts or principles of reason. It holds a more intense poetic energy, a greater compression of passion, than does Dryden's Zimri: that glows, this is white-hot. Dryden draws a real man, but Pope distills, compresses, and ejects through one per-

[1] For a closer discussion of Sporus as a dissociated personality, see *Christ and Nietzsche*, IV, 125.

son, the living essence of a whole poisoned society. Sporus, set between Shakespeare's Lucio and Byron's Steno, is a poetic archetype.

The creation is paradoxical, since its very intensity is set to constitute a condemnation of not-being: Sporus is vigorously inactive and powerfully a nothing. The lively essences are, of course, Pope's, and these are strongly emotional. Had the condemnation depended on pure reasoning rather than on an analytic impressionism it would have cut across the poet's own human understanding as expressed in his *Epistle to Lord Cobham*.[1] The emotional and sensory nature, the personal and relative quality, of the portrait tend to save it from certain charges, since there is no claim to a dispassionate consideration. The feeling is directed against a person, or society, not being properly itself, and the more cool, less sensory, yet equally unreasoned, scalpel, incisiveness of the Atticus analysis earlier, being a study of insincerity, lukewarmness, and petty pride, is at root a similar indictment. Both, being creations drawn from real persons, are, as such, scarcely charitable, and we may find it difficult to isolate a purely receptive and imaginative understanding. Yet we can never exactly know the provocation, and any final judgement on the original situation must, it seems, include information of a subtle sort quite impossible to obtain. All fiction has its germ in personal experience, and Lord Hervey may well have provided merely a release-moment to a piled-up disgust of society as a whole, like the bursting of a dam. The compressed venom resembles that of Shakespeare's final period, and substantially the same experience is being transmitted. Conditions now force, or at least allow, a shameless, to us it seems a libellous, directness of reference: the context is different, but Pope is perhaps no more to be blamed than Shakespeare. For all we know there may have been living originals of Osric and Oswald —or Caliban!

The *Epistle to Dr. Arbuthnot* itself gives us Pope's most comprehensive defence:

> *Curst be the verse, how well soe'er it flow,*
> *That tends to make one worthy man my foe.*
>
> (283)

Here and elsewhere he is quite certain of his rectitude. This epistle shows a blend of violence and gentleness, varying between attack and pathos, social criticism and autobiography, swelling and subsiding

[1] *Moral Essays*, I.

with an undulatory movement, whose balance repays attention. His chief boasts, of looking after his mother to the last and cherishing a deep friendship, are not those of a misanthrope: he is never submerged by his own satire, but well above it. He may have been mistaken in actual judgements—how can any man be certain of another's worthiness or knavery?—but his personal reactions are being used as the explosive force behind a satire which becomes elsewhere a quite general indictment. I believe a final understanding will acquit him of unnecessary cruelty, though it might have to be couched in intellectual terms which his more intuitive sense of his own righteousness need not have taken into account. Anyway, his persons are today as fictional as Iago and Cloten, and the writing indisputatably holds the kind of integrity needed for great poetry. I ask that we bring such a view to a short inspection of Pope's *Imitations of Horace* (1733–8). Such a view is at least fictionally forced, since these epistles, like that to Arbuthnot, sometimes dramatize the poet himself, showing him in a favourable light.

They enjoy a strange agility and happy freedom, together with a strangely non-sensuous appeal and a vivid use of abstract nouns; a continual, if reserved, nature-reference helping to preserve the usual Shakespearian kinship. They are often dramatic with a dialogue structure showing Pope's discussion with some friend on his own position as satirist. Dissatisfaction with his calling alternates with sublimation of it, the central stimulus being at once a general irritation and a happy sense of power. Though he knows himself part of the process he deplores, the loss of contact, the flinging apart of ideals and actions, literature and life; though he is forced back continually on discussion of great writers or himself instead of other heroisms; yet now his ethical mission grows clearer and his verse becomes more sinewy, purposive and fast. As dynamic ideals are pitted against a putrefying society, so the language, like that of Shakespeare's later style, is continually at work to transmute living essence into a compact yet lightning phraseology, as in the pith and pregnancy and mastery of the abstract and universal in 'puff'd prosperity',[1] or

> *Oh Impudence of wealth! with all thy store*
> *How dar'st thou let one worthy man be poor?*
>
> (*Horace*, *Sat.* II, ii, 117)

[1] *Horace*, *Sat.* II, ii, 126.

These vast yet feather-light abstractions flash like a club: 'prosperity', 'impudence'; or again, 'violence', 'antipathy' (as on p. 76 below). Pope fights material inertia with a spiritual energy, aiming to inject poetic vitality into the communal mind without any reliance on fiction.

These self-dramatizing epistles are as little negative as *Timon of Athens*, a play which covers Pope's major attacks. There the positive, the purposeful direction, is in the hero; here in Pope himself. He becomes his own protagonist, and separate satiric thrusts are subsidiary to discussion of their own nature and necessity. Having followed his own teaching in Epistle II of the *Essay on Man* by trusting those ruling and envenomed passions that can simultaneously create a Sporus, he also rises beyond them, mounts on his own emotions, brings his whole self to the launching of a less personal, yet even more virulent, attack. The sublimated emotion, though continuous with the other, is qualitatively different, the expression less sensuous and the emotion impersonal:

Farewell then Verse, and Love, and ev'ry Toy,
The Rhymes and Rattles of the Man or Boy;
What right, what true, what fit we justly call,
Let this be all my care—for this is All.

(*Horace, Ep.* I, i, 17)

He feels newly grown up, and his poetry takes on a Pauline fervour, the new inclusiveness making his earlier work seem to him, though not necessarily to us, comparatively weak. There is a delighted excitement, with a corresponding lessening of personal hostility, his interlocutor sometimes interrupting to create a subtle humour. The impersonality is one with the drama. He is now more interested in himself as satirist than in any satire, but only because he is presenting himself as a dramatized universal, as the voice of a communal vitality divorced from the community. This, the objective viewing of his own vital direction, is the true gist of the little dramas. They are therefore in essence positive and impersonal.

The explicit attacks continue as before against luxury and corruption, with usual reminders of temperance and simplicity. Commercial enterprise has become a mad race for wealth at whatever physical risks,[1] flattery has undermined Church teaching[2] and

[1] *Horace, Ep.* I, i, 67–72.
[2] Ibid., II, ii, 218–25.

letters.[1] Crown and politics are alike corrupt.[2] The old aristocracy has fallen before a new order of 'booby' lords.[3] So

In Soldier, Churchman, Patriot, Man in Pow'r,
'Tis Av'rice all, Ambition is no more!
(*Epilogue* I, 161)

The throne itself is vigorously attacked, especially in the *Epistle to Augustus*, where the old thought of England as a dominating and central influence recurs with ironic intention.[4] The swing-over from Elizabethan royalism to the piercing revolutionary visions of the early nineteenth century pivots on Pope's work. He writes of war like Byron:

. . . let Jove encrust
Swords, pikes and guns, with everlasting rust!
Peace is my dear delight. . . .
(*Horace, Sat.* II, i, 73)

His 'Yes, the last Pen for Freedom let me draw' [5] suggests that pen to be rather the first of a new, than the last of an old, order.

Since the main complaints date back at least to the New Testament, though as far from satisfaction now as then, they are not in themselves so important as is their vigour of transmission. Besides, the aim is towards an emotional redirection more fundamental than any specific teaching. Certainly what Pope regards as ugly, stupid, evil, or what not is, to any right-thinking person, ugly, stupid, and evil. There is no indecision: ethical fervour and imaginative virility are co-active in as sure and indissoluble a partnership as you will find anywhere. But the vigour *is* the teaching. That is why personal disgusts must still be allowed reference, and Pope refuses to limit himself to attack on abstract sins,[6] since that lets slip the very dynamic he would exploit. The concentration on such is itself a danger: the 'fear' of desiring advancement as bad as the desire, since each equally argue an admiration;[7] and this is not to be cured by any thinking, by any static doctrine. No attack is levelled against obvious crime. The dispute seems to involve an essence at once more than mental and less than instinctive: 'a fool quite angry' is 'quite

[1] *Horace, Sat.* II, i, 21–2.
[2] *Epilogue*, I, 105–10.
[3] *Horace, Sat.* II, ii, 175–6.
[4] *Horace, Ep.* II, i, 394–419.
[5] *Epilogue*, II, 248.
[6] Ibid., II, 13.
[7] *Horace, Ep.* I, vi, 18–21.

innocent' in the *Epistle to Dr. Arbuthnot* (107). Purposive vitality gets respect: it is the test of highest poetry.[1] After all, Pope had praised Sir John Blunt in a difficult passage[2] for rationalizing a 'ruling passion' into a mad scheme, with sharp condemnation of purposelessness, even though purpose be taken to 'extremes'. This comes during a discussion of the motives and rationalizations of avarice,[3] where the subtleties involved force a treatment in personal and narrative terms. Pope's ultimate gospel is not reducible to a static logic, and must be referred to the dynamic psychology in Epistle II of the *Essay on Man*. In both this and his doctrine of the universal balance and 'power',[4] he draws close to the teaching of Nietzsche.[5]

The poetry, though tense with passion, is always superbly at ease. There is a white purity as well as a white fury. It is, indeed, itself happy, with a gay variation, showing often a delightful friendship in the manner of address, with diction chatty, forceful, amiable, and resonant, by turns. Separate lines exert a stripped athletic grace, as in the clean action of, 'The devil is in you if you cannot dine',[6] or 'The worst of madmen is a saint run mad'.[7] There is a Shakespearian control of vast concepts, as in this reminiscence of *Troilus and Cressida* followed by one of Pope's new running lucidities:

This subtle Thief of life, this paltry Time,
What will it leave me if it snatch my rhyme?
(*Horace, Ep.* II, ii, 76)

A darker, though no less brave, cosmic apprehension than that of the *Essay on Man* draws him now closer to *King Lear*:

This Vault of Air, this congregated Ball,
Self-center'd Sun, and Stars that rise and fall,
There are, my Friend! whose philosophic eyes
Look thro', and trust the Ruler with his skies,
To him commit the hour, the day, the year,
And view this dreadful All without a fear.
(*Horace, Ep.* I, vi, 5)

[1] Ibid., II, i, 338–47.
[2] *Moral Essays*, III, 151–62.
[3] Attacked at *Horace, Ep.* I, i, 65–84.
[4] *Moral Essays*, III, 159–68.
[5] The complexities of Pope's ethical thinking forecast Nietzsche's, and for a further elucidation I must point to my analysis of *Thus Spake Zarathustra* in *Christ and Nietzsche* (V).
[6] *Horace, Sat.* II, ii, 148.
[7] *Horace, Ep.* I, vi, 27.

See the careless handling, the reckless poetic out-tossing, of immensities together with the new intensity shadowed of a *Macbeth* fear, as again in the solemn meditations of his epistle to Colonel Cotterell:

Does neither Rage inflame, nor Fear appal?
Not the black fear of death, that saddens all?
With terrors round, can Reason hold her throne,
Despise the known, nor tremble at th' unknown?
Survey both worlds, intrepid and entire,
In spite of witches, devils, dreams and fire?
Pleas'd to look forward, pleas'd to look behind,
And count each birth-day with a grateful mind?
(*Horace, Ep.* II, ii, 308)

We may leap the centuries to find a quatrain of Byronic detonation:

Say, does thy blood rebel, thy bosom move
With wretched Av'rice, or as wretched Love?
Know, there are Words, and Spells, which can control
Between the Fits this Fever of the soul.
(*Horace, Ep.* I, i, 55)

The word music is precisely one with meaning: it is rather a vibrancy than a music. There are swinging blows and hammering repetitions. The couplets break free of old constraints, they ripple, ring, dance, volley, joke, and reverberate, using a whole armoury of technical resource; scatter a hail of monosyllables, tilt with alliteration. Scorn of militaristic heroisms rolls out in the heavy ironic assonance of

Rend with tremendous sound your ears asunder,
With Gun, Drum, Trumpet, Blunderbuss, and Thunder . . .
(*Horace, Sat.* II, i, 25)

Or equal scorn is meted to Miltonic excellences of

Gold, Silver, Iv'ry, Vases sculptur'd high,
Paint, Marble, Gems, and robes of Persian dye . . .
(*Horace, Ep.* II, ii, 264)

Pope's own mind runs rather to nature and man than to inventions, crafts, and arts. But a different appreciation, together with hint of an earlier style, murmurs in the delicate fervency of 'Then Marble, softened into life, grew warm'.[1]

[1] *Horace, Ep.* II, i, 147.

The best strength does not show itself in short quotation, but rather in paragraphs, where couplet-modulation is malleable as in any Shakespearian sequence, a muscular cohesion rippling vertically down the page. Such evolve organically, couplet answers couplet, as in the run-on movements of the conclusion to the epistle to Bolingbroke.[1] The dialogue form may assist delightful humour as at the conclusion to the epistle to Mr. Fortescue,[2] or the split line-units and tennis-ball toss and return within and across the couplet in the second *Epilogue*, 10–27. Pope's humour is never unhealthy, never itself cruel, though on occasion he himself is: nor is it ever far off.

There is no bitterness, since at every instance there is creative direction, but neither is there any weakening of scorn. He would 'cure the arrant'st Puppy of his Pride',[3] and plant a scorching, branding impress:

> *Yes, while I live, no rich or noble knave*
> *Shall walk the World, in credit, to his grave.*
>
> (*Horace, Sat.* II, i, 119)

Yet all must be felt as flotsam on the torrent of the one forthright passion. He answers objections from an impregnable ethic: if a distasteful image turns your stomach, so, he replies, 'does Flattery mine'[4]. His calling is one of national importance, 'useful to the state' as any soldier's,[5] provided that it does not sink to praise of some 'monster of a king', or turn virtue or religion to sport.[6] In straight-line development from *Windsor Forest*, Pope's patriotism is no whit abated, though now his 'country's ruin' makes him 'grave'.[7] Friends recognize and acknowledge his integrity; [8] they are dramatized as warning him against the dangers that must certainly have been risked,[9] but he insists on driving his attacks far beyond personal animosities against people in high position against whom he has, as an individual, no possible complaint,[10] following only 'Virtue' and her friends,[11] indebted, 'thanks to Homer', to 'no Prince or Peer alive'.[12] Enjoying a brave independence won by his pen, he feels that pen as a pistol,[13] or a sword,[14] and satire a 'sacred weapon'.[15] Grouping St. Paul with Aristippus, he acknowledges no final intellectual

[1] Ibid., I, i, 161–88.
[2] *Horace, Sat.* II, i, 143–56.
[3] *Horace, Ep.* I, i, 60.
[4] *Epilogue*, II, 182.
[5] *Horace, Ep.* II, i, 204.
[6] Ibid., i, 210–11.
[7] *Epilogue*, II, 207.
[8] *Horace, Sat.* II, i, 138.
[9] Ibid., i, 101–4.
[10] *Epilogue*, II, 157–67.
[11] *Horace, Sat.* II, i, 121.
[12] *Horace, Ep.* II, ii, 69.
[13] *Horace, Sat.* II, i, 105.
[14] *Epilogue*, II, 248.
[15] Ibid., 212.

authorities except 'righteousness',[1] and that 'priestless Muse' which preserves good men with fire caught from her 'shrine', and opens the 'Temple of Eternity'.[2]

So a happy valiancy, a buoyancy and triumphing certitude, ring from a confidence resting on 'the strong Antipathy of Good to Bad'.[3] Though he is surely too bold, trusts too uncompromisingly in a human intuition, and thus himself incurs the charge of pride, he makes of his answer at once a final defence and a further thrust:

Yes, I am proud; I must be proud to see
Men not afraid of God, afraid of me.
(*Epilogue*, II, 208)

He is proud, as St. Paul is proud, with a righteous, because now wholly impersonal, intolerance. The lines speak with a vigour and transparency of syntax deriving from the simplicity and force of the indictment. The teaching is never static, since that is the way to a thousand self-deceptions, mistaking the 'reverse of wrong for right'.[4] The burning sincerity of a more dynamic gospel is implicit throughout these epistles and shines in their very militancy. His aim is single: to set 'the *Passions* on the side of Truth',[5] and take Heaven by 'Violence of Song'.[6]

The keen religious fervency that projects itself into such phrases as 'virtue', 'Heaven', 'priestless Muse', 'Temple of Eternity', these last coming, as a climax, in the second *Epilogue* (234–5), may recall Pope's own early *Dying Christian to his Soul* (1712), his *Messiah* (1712), and *The Temple of Fame* (1711–1715), a poem deserving close attention for its vital and spiritualized use of the architectural. These poems stand slightly apart from Pope's naturalistic development. But in the *Messiah* the divine is itself a super-sun: there was never a final antagonism. In Milton a great force turns inwards, becomes rigid; in Pope an original gentleness widens to an overpowering prophetic challenge. His life-work shows a steady expanding, a flowering, of natural impulse into the ethical fervour of the Horatian satires. Nor must we forget his *Universal Prayer* (1738), which states the centre and circumference of his doctrine.

[1] *Horace, Ep.* I, i, 23–34.
[2] *Epilogue*, II, 232–5.
[3] Ibid., II, 198.
[4] *Moral Essays*, III, 198.
[5] *Horace, Ep.* II, i, 218.
[6] Ibid., i, 240.

III

SYMBOLIC ETERNITIES:

An Introduction to 'The Temple of Fame'

III. SYMBOLIC ETERNITIES

I

At the conclusion to our last essay we referred to *The Temple of Fame* with its 'vital and spiritualized use of the architectural'. This is Pope's only poem to concentrate at length on works of spatial artistry, and a separate treatment of it is needed.

This is not his normal *genre*. He was interested in the laws of architecture,[1] but as a poet he generally preserves a direct and unmediated approach to the human problem, whether in fiction, psychological diagnosis or satire, eschewing all facile symbols of transcendence and leaving the harmonizing and eternalizing to diction and couplet. His instinctive interests are nature and man; he has none of the previous century's delight in gadgets and artefacts. Too exact a formality in gardens or house-design repelled him, and he had little mercy on a nobleman's grounds full of 'trees cut to statues' and 'statues thick as trees' [2]; and he could write of metallic arts with scorn.[3] His poetry is not, any more than Shakespeare's or Byron's, dominated by other arts. And yet their *vitalities* fascinated him. In *Windsor Forest* he could endue 'a new Whitehall' with visionary meaning, and see 'temples' rising as 'the beauteous works of Peace' (378–80); he could compose the exquisite line, 'Then marble, soften'd into life, grew warm' [4]; and see the 'priestless Muse' opening the 'Temple of Eternity'.[5] He was interested in the new landscape gardening, columns, terraces and all, provided that it was a true collaboration of art and nature, as at Stowe.[6] He was himself a practitioner and innovator, making his own grounds at Twickenham a model, and devoting himself for many years to the artistry

[1] Tillotson, quoting Spence, 'Design', 95.
[2] *Moral Essays*, IV: see p. 66.
[3] *Horace, Ep.* II, ii, 264; see p. 74 above.
[4] *Horace, Ep.* II, i, 147.
[5] *Sat., Epilogue*, II, 235.
[6] *Moral Essays*, I, 47–70.

of his Grotto. He painted, too. Of his youthful experience as a painter and his passionate concern, both in poetry and in painting, for colour, Norman Ault has recently given us a valuable account, quoting his lines (1714–17) to Charles Jervas, his art-master:

> *Smit with the love of Sister-Arts we came,*
> *And met congenial, mingling flame with flame;*
> *Like friendly colours found them both unite,*
> *And each from each contract new strength and light.*

Thus smitten, they will tread together 'th' Eternal Alpine Snow', Pope's image for man's furthest endeavour, as in the *Essay on Criticism*.[1] So their track is pursued 'from art to art'.[2] Like Blake and Rossetti, Pope served both arts, glimpsing a wondrous possibility in their union; and in his address to Addison (1715–21) called for a revival of sculpture, honoured equally with poetry (51–8). The lines to Jervas have already been referred by Professor Tillotson to *The Temple of Fame*, in the *Twickenham* edition (1940; 231). But this artistic marriage raises so many fascinating questions that we must preface our discussion of the longer poem by a review of such symbolic fusions in the work of other poets. Without such a preparation, the peculiar importance of Pope's contribution cannot be assessed.

II

All art may be defined as the attempt to fuse 'space' with 'time'. Music and literature exist primarily in time, as sequences; sculpture, painting, and architecture, in space. But this is not the whole story. Each aims to transcend its limitations in space-time. Thus the temporal arts attain 'form' or 'structure', and are rich with all those meanings which I have regularly defined as 'spatial', while the spatial arts tend to suggest narrative, or at least to hold some vital significance that trembles on the brink of motion[3]; or again, even when this is least obvious, as in architecture, it is clear that they need time, as Byron observes when writing of St. Peter's in *Childe Harold* (IV, 153–9), for their mental reception.

[1] *Essay on Criticism*, 232; and compare the 'eternal snows' of *The Temple of Fame*, 57.

[2] *New Light on Pope* (1949); v, 72–3. These last phrases are quoted from an early, and in parts, it seems, superior, draft of the poem.

[3] For a modern analysis of the process, see Sir Herbert Read's *The Meaning of Art* (1931, Pelican edn. 1949); paras. 22, 26*a*.

Music speaks to the ear and painting to the eye; but single senses give us glimpses only, and the reality may be supposed to correspond rather to whatever might be reported by all the senses, if such could be, working in artistic unison. Nor have we any reason to suppose that it would be exhausted by that. It is best to admit frankly that all art is necessarily inadequate, since the super-sensuous reality cannot be captured and held by our minds; but it remains a valid approximation. The greater reality is not, however, to be supposed as in opposition to sense experience, but rather as some richer dimension of that experience: it exists in the eternal dimension, which contains, and surpasses, time, but it is not to be thought of as static: it exists in space-time. Space-time is eternity, and art an approximation to its expression.

The 'interpretation' of art must therefore be called more than ancillary; it is rather, as has always been recognized in practice, however often denied in theory, a needed auxiliary. It will, moreover, be clear that such interpretations inevitably tend to concentrate on the spatial properties of a temporal art and the temporal properties, as in Lessing's and Ruskin's interest in the moving qualities of painting, of a spatial art. Interpretation assists the art under discussion to say more clearly what it is aiming to say, but cannot quite say, though it does suggest, by reason of its own peculiar limitation.[1]

There have been, of course, attempts in every age to harmonize various arts into some greater and more inclusive art: such is the attempt of opera, of ballet, the music dramas of Wagner, and certain interesting modern advances by the cinema. But, though the blend of music, poetry, and ritual dance appears to have attained a high measure of success in the drama of the ancients, our modern attempts generally leave something to be desired, since we find either that one art tends to dominate at the expense, and sometimes to the serious indignity, of the rest; or that, even when all are working together, the mind cannot assimilate more than is contained in artistic experiences of a simpler kind. This is no reason for giving up the attempt, and we may expect future developments of greater achievement.

Poetry, with its extension in Shakespearian drama, has perhaps come as near as may be, for us today, to a wholly satisfying inclusion. All writing, as Joseph Conrad tells us in his preface to *The Nigger*

[1] For my own methods, see *Essays in Criticism*, Oct., 1953 and April, 1954; also my *Shakespearian Production* (enlarged 1964) throughout.

of the Narcissus, 'must strenuously aspire to the plasticity of sculpture, to the colour of painting, and to the magic suggestiveness of music'. Poetry in particular offers an experience which is mysteriously both sound and colour, time and space: music, imagery, and meaning are often inextricably entwined, almost identical, and in it we have the heart of our mystery. Sometimes, as pre-eminently in a great speech of Shelley's *Prometheus Unbound*,[1] it deliberately plays on a confusion of sense-impressions (e.g., in Shelley, 'the music of the living grass and air', IV, iv, 257) to crash the barrier shutting man's sense-locked consciousness from what lies beyond. Nevertheless poetry is, in hard fact, a temporal art, composed of sequences in logic and narrative, its spatial qualities being only spatial by metaphor; they are, to use a paradox, inwardly and spiritually spatial. It is therefore the especial business of interpretation to wrest the deeper meanings from its various patterns in rhyme and stanza, its colourings, its half-visualized scenes, its massing of associations, its structure. We have already seen (p. 53) how Pope's *Essay on Man* exists less as a logical proposition, or set of logically cohering propositions, than through a juxtaposition of contradictory philosophies to make a greater, beyond-philosophy, statement: it is the work of a man with the mind-structure of a poet using philosophic sequences for his purpose. There is here a vital distinction, which applies also to poetic interpretation, since interpretation does not reduce poetry to philosophy, but rather uses philosophic thinking to assist our responses to a comprehension that philosophic thought alone could never attain, and might even have to repudiate; the comprehension, that is, of what the work of poetry is striving, and no art can do more, to realize. It gives the poetry spatial projection, puts it, inwardly, on the stage of our imaginations, *produces* it for us. We all know how a work in dramatic form may reveal unsuspected riches under visual and spatial projection: interpretation merely extends the process to poetry in general.

It is often observed that the importance of a work of art lies not in what it says, but in what it *is*. But poetry clearly says something too; and since a work of art is an organic whole, what it says must be related very closely to what it is. That Shelley should choose to write of the skylark and Keats of the nightingale had something to do with the bright-ethereal and dark-woodland qualities of their respective manners. We could, indeed, define poetry as 'an arrange-

[1] IV, iv, 236–69; *The Starlit Dome* (1941), III, 219–23.

ment of words which is what it says'; or, put the other way, 'which is always saying the reality which it is'. Therefore, since, as we have seen, poetry is a space-time reality, we shall not be surprised to find it offering, with what might be called a kind of introspective self-consciousness, a number of precise symbolisms of the space-time dimension which it exists to embody. These symbols I have already, in various works, discussed in detail, but a short retrospective re-grouping and commentary will prove a helpful preliminary to our study of *The Temple of Fame.*

The Christian Trinity itself might, in its fusion of unity with diversity, its dramatic formation, be called an archetype of all such symbolisms. It is as a living and ceaselessly interacting, yet ever-still, complexity in self-union, and in Dante's *Divina Commedia* the central mysteries of the faith are presented in similarly paradoxical terms involving fusions of action with harmony, duality with unity, and so on; as in descriptions of the Gryphon, of Beatrice, in the circular schemes used throughout, and in the final vision of the human form set within the divine 'circling'.[1]

Renaissance poetry is often found to speak through a number of related symbolisms in attempt to blend the arts of space and time within some highly charged unit. These we may for simplicity group under two main headings, human and transcendental—the word perhaps says too much, but there is none better—as: (i) the action-pose, and (ii) musical buildings.

Shakespeare has comparatively little to offer in description of the visual arts, though the Sonnets use the eternal connotations of monumental architecture to point a negative; both *The Merchant of Venice* (III, ii, 114–18) and *Timon of Athens* (I, i, 31–9) offer descriptions of motion within painting; and significant sculptural miniatures occur in the Final Plays, as with Marina called 'a palace for the crown'd Truth to dwell in' and compared with 'Patience gazing on kings' graves' to outface 'extremity'.[2] Shakespeare's main symbols, corresponding roughly to our two divisions, human and transcendental, are: (i) the King, or the Crown, and (ii) Tempests and Music. For the rest, I would point here to two peculiarly relevant occasions. The first is Hamlet's address to the Players,[3] on the knife-edge balance of power with control, of action with grace, to attain

[1] *The Christian Renaissance* (enlarged 1962): VII, 99–105; XII, 229–32.

[2] *Pericles*, V, i, 123, 140: and see *The Winter's Tale*, V, ii, 107; *Cymbeline*, II, iv, 72–85, 89; *The Crown of Life* (1947), II, 64–5; III, 118; IV, 174–6. [3] *Hamlet*, III, ii.

artistic poise; a passage which must be understood in direct relation to the play's central problem.[1] The second is the coming to life of Hermione's statue in *The Winter's Tale*, with all its sharp underlining in the dialogue of the space-time paradoxes being enacted, to make what might be called an extreme development of the 'action-pose'.

Statues are always likely to assume importance in humanistic poetry. Byron has some valuable statue-descriptions in *Childe Harold* (IV, 49–53; 160–3; the *Venus*, the *Laocoön*, and the *Apollo*), seeing the sculptor's art as an incarnation of the divine, and noticing in one of them its moment of action ('the shaft hath just been shot'); a yet finer tribute to the 'divine' import of the 'poesy' within the 'kindled' brow of sculpture occurs in *The Prophecy of Dante* (IV); and he has left us some interesting prose comments on the art.[2] The symbolic heart of *Marino Faliero* is an equestrian statue (III, i). The use of plastic suggestion to print eternal significances on his human delineation becomes emphatic in Byron's latest work. There are examples in *Sardanapalus*, and in *Don Juan* they abound. The poem's delicate feeling is concerned throughout with 'the precious porcelain of human clay' (IV, 11), surely never more exquisitely realized in poetry than in the lines:

> *A pure, transparent, pale, yet radiant face,*
> *Like to a lighted alabaster vase.*
>
> (VIII, 96)

Juan and Haidée are imaged as a statue group (II, 194); Aurora is spiritualized by descriptions on the brink of sculpture and specifically related to the eternal (XV, 43–7; 58); the ghostly paintings of Norman Abbey are alive with poignant meanings (XVI, 19); and at the poem's climax, through a fine stroke of metaphysical humour, we discover that the mysterious figure thought to be a ghost, and at one point sculpturally conceived, is a warmly living, and amorous, duchess (XVI, 120–3). Throughout *Don Juan*, as was shown at length in *The Burning Oracle*, the clustering sculptural impressions serve to impart some feeling of eternal essences, or significances, within the poem's keenly visualized descriptions.

The other great Romantics, though in their main emphases less humanistic, were nevertheless sensitive to the eternal, space-time,

[1] '*Hamlet* Reconsidered', *The Wheel of Fire*, 1949 edn.

[2] The Bowles Controversy, LJ, V, 547–51, 557. For the Bowles Controversy, see pp. 113, 137 below.

properties of the action-pose. Wordsworth's description of Newton's statue with its prism and silent face, as

The marble index of a mind for ever
Voyaging through strange seas of Thought, alone
(*The Prelude*, III, 62)

is unforgettable. Andreas, the blazing centre of Coleridge's *Zapolya*, is described in statued action:

So looks the statue, in our hall, o' the god,
The shaft just flown that killed the serpent.
(I, i, 258)

The god is Apollo: Coleridge may have been thinking of the same statue, the Apollo Belvedere, as was Byron. Shelley's transcendental intuitions in *Prometheus Unbound* find expression through a remarkable description of chariot-figures whose very speed appears, under poetic pressure, to freeze them in a living stillness; and there are descriptions of wondrous palaces richly engraved with 'Praxitelean shapes' and 'Phidian forms'.[1] Keats' poetry works continually through what I have called 'tip-toe' effects, little pictures of poised motion, his *Ode on a Grecian Urn*, with its action snapshots of passionate humanity for ever fixed within a rondure equating beauty with truth to make a neat miniature of Dante's final vision, offering the most obvious example of a general tendency.[2]

In Browning's *The Statue and the Bust* we have a satiric opposition of statue-forms against the dynamic of human existence, though *Pippa Passes* shows a fine insight into the vitalities of sculpture. Opposite views of painting are presented in *Andrea del Sarto* and *Fra Lippo Lippi*, and *all* the arts work together in *Cleon*, in direct relation to life, death, and immortality. The statue-piece of the Resurrection central to Ibsen's last work *When We Dead Awaken* recalls *The Winter's Tale*, and the dialogue at key moments plays on and into the most subtle and secret balances of art and life.[3] Living statuary is an important element in the semi-transcendental humanism of Shaw's *Back to Methuselah*; and the 'phantom' of Yeats' *Resurrection* is similarly conceived. A modern poem of first importance, Francis Berry's *The Iron Christ*, specifically defines the attainment of a harmony beyond war in terms of a giant effigy of Christ

[1] *Prometheus Unbound*, II, iv, 129–40; III, iii, 161–6; III, iv, 108–21; *The Starlit Dome*, III, 205, 214–15.

[2] *The Starlit Dome*, IV, 294–6.

[3] *Ibsen* (1962), VII, 98–106.

hauled with great labour up the Andes, and gradually, precariously, hoisted and tilted into position to reach a balanced and lasting poise upon the heights.[1] Poise and peace are inter-affective and inter-illuminating concepts.

So much for our 'action-pose'. Next, we have our 'musical buildings'. In *The Burning Oracle* I discussed Milton's poetry in terms of his passion for artefacts and music in *disjunction*, his solids being static and cold in proportion as his music is overpowering. But there is a noble union within the cathedral description of *Il Penseroso*, and *Paradise Lost* shows at least three notable successes. One is the massing of Satan's hosts into a solid array which next moves lightly to flute music, the power of this particular description helping us to understand the universal meaning of pageantry and processions; the next is the building of a great structure by organ-music, the music being conceived as the building power; and the third, the creation of the world to the accompaniment of song and music.[2]

Such symbolisms are developed by the Romantics, whose insight delights to express itself, as Shakespeare's does not, in the vertical dimension. So we have our mountains, domes and temples. Our most compact unit is Coleridge's *Kubla Khan* with its mystic and marvellous dome once glimpsed and now only to be built with the aid of the Abyssinian girl's music in 'air', or poetry. It is a musical, poetic, transcendental dome, contrasted with the river of life and nature generally; the solid and stable with the fluid. Wordsworth's life-work shows a gradual shift from nature-poetry to works describing the arts of design, and edifices in especial; and in his preface to *The Excursion* he described his life-work as a cathedral, with ante-chapels. His most striking symbolic successes in this *genre* are probably the 'imperial palace' of his *Immortality Ode* and the fine comparison of dawn on the clouds and mountains to a number of palatial fabrics all 'molten together', in *The Excursion* (II, 831–60). Shelley's poetry is full of domes, of which 'life' as a 'dome' refracting 'eternity' in *Adonais* is the best known; and he has temples too, to which his paradoxical rivers flow *up*; and there is his marvellous passage already mentioned (p. 82) in which a confusion of impressions intermingles nature with orbs, spheres, and even axles to 'drown the sense'.[3] Such mechanisms help us to understand the peculiar nature of

[1] Francis Berry's collected poems, *The Galloping Centaur*, Methuen, 1952.

[2] *Paradise Lost*, I, 531–71; I, 705–17; VII, 252–60, 557–640.

[3] *Prometheus Unbound*, IV, iv, 236–61.

Keats' poetic magic flowering from a moment-by-moment fusion of the opposites in play. His buildings, interiors (as in *The Eve of St. Agnes*), urns (in the odes *On Indolence* and *On a Grecian Urn*) are warm with human vitalities, and his trees sculptural; nature, man, and art are intrinsicate and each at every instant endowed with the properties of the others. We have a fine example of a magical building flowering into creation, with a 'haunting music' as sole supporter of its 'faery roof', in *Lamia* (II, 119–41). Wordsworth is eminently a poet of *sound* and wrote an ode 'On the *Power* of Sound'. The symbolisms of these four poets are discussed throughout *The Starlit Dome*.

Byron takes a similar course in his own different manner. In aesthetic theory he supports the rights of architecture as against nature,[1] and uses architectural metaphors as when he compares Pope's work to a Greek temple, to establish his poetic and political judgements (see pp. 148, 150 below). He was fascinated by the definition of architecture as 'frozen music', and anxious to discover its origin.[2] In *Childe Harold* (IV, 156) he extends himself in description of St. Peter's in Rome, 'all musical in its immensities'; his handling of Venetian architecture in *Marino Faliero* (III, i; IV, i) is dramatically and atmospherically important; and so is his wonderful realization of Norman Abbey, on whose ruins the winds harp an 'unearthly' and mysterious music beneath the moon recalling Butler's *Erewhon*, in *Don Juan* (XIII, 55–74).

The meaning of our many 'musical buildings' is most clearly set down in Browning's *Abt Vogler*, where the experience of the eternal dimension reached by and through the musician's art is exactly, and in detail, described as a throwing up of a palatial structure; and in *An Epistle of Karshish* this dimension becomes a 'vast distracting orb' around time's 'meagre thread'.

Old legends tell of cities built by music,[3] the thought being recaptured by Tennyson's *Tithonus*:

> *. . . that strange song I heard Apollo sing*
> *When Ilion, like a mist, rose into towers.*

[1] The Bowles Controversy, LJ, 546–8, 552. See pp. 138–9, below.

[2] Journal, 17 Nov., 1813; LJ, II, 326.

[3] Compare my remarks on the magical properties of music in *The Shakespearian Tempest*, VI. We must remember always that music, like thunder, is a Shakespearian *power*, and accompanies the resurrections in *Pericles* and *The Winter's Tale*. Note, too, the title of Wordsworth's Ode above.

You get it again in O'Shaughnessy's 'We are the music makers', wherein 'great cities' are said to be builded by poetry:

We, in the ages lying
In the buried past of the earth,
Built Nineveh with our sighing,
And Babel itself in our mirth . . .

Yeats' man-transcending 'starlit' or 'moonlit' dome in *Byzantium*, which may suggest the dome of the heavens as well as a building, for all human domes imitate the sky, is associated with the music, if such we can call it, of the 'great cathedral gong'. As a climax to our story we have Francis Berry's *Fall of a Tower*, throughout constructed round an exact use of these symbols, its theme reaching fulfilment in the building of a Temple blending Sun-worship with Christianity to the music of violins and flutes:

A spiral-fluted Temple with a Dome
Of patterned glass to take the varying shine
Between the green far hills and crystal seas.

This particular example of our recurring symbol is remarkable for its easy compacting of a number of meanings, natural, human and divine.

Architecture, springing from king and ancestor worship and the will to establish for them cenotaphs and memorials, asserts the vertical against the horizontal, flowers into the eternal meanings of temple and cathedral, and finally embeds itself in poetic symbolism. Shakespeare's use of monuments in the Sonnets and 'king's graves' in *Pericles* (v, i, 140) provides a good commentary on the process.

Metaphysical poetry shows a dearth of such major symbols, since its concern with the eternal dimension is conceptually explicit. It uses whatever minor conceits or images come to mind, and counters its transcendental themes with colloquial rhythms and vocabulary, so reversing the usual process whereby a poet eternalizes a realistic theme with pattern, music, and symbol.

Though metaphysical in sympathy, Eliot's work is also rich in the romantic tradition. Thinking of our two divisions, human and transcendental, I would select: (i) *La Figlia che Piange*, as good an example as we shall find of Eliot's skilful use of feather-light balances in image and thought, here serving a sculptural centre of momentary poise to mark a choice and divergence of the ways; and (ii) the *Four*

Quartets, so rich in meditation on different varieties of time and that which is beyond time, and in the balanced identities of motion and stillness, of action and inaction (*Burnt Norton, The Dry Salvages*), to create a vital eternity; also expressed by the thought of words reaching the 'silence' through their patterned form or music (*Burnt Norton*), and of music itself heard so deeply 'that it is not heard at all' (*The Day Salvages*); by various symbols of dance (*Burnt Norton, Little Gidding*), and by the Chinese vase moving 'perpetually' in its own 'stillness' (*Burnt Norton*). Eliot and Francis Berry stand as our two finest modern exponents of the symbols we are discussing.

Our brief account may be summed up by a couple of prose quotations from my own *Atlantic Crossing*. Here is the first:

'And in wider issues too, you must, in order to be true to the surface of life, work from some universal centre: not a static centre, but a centre which is itself movement. A rhythmic centre, or heart. You must find the centre not of a static pattern alone, but of the unfurling movement of patterns; not the outward brilliance, but the inward core of music, the ship's throbbing engines, the blood-infusing and colour-shooting heart. You must aim to know the patterned growing and musical petal-design, the pulsating solidity, of the flower-building you would create.'

(VII, 214)

And here is the other:

'But it is a moving, developing pattern, its colours fed from inward wells of passionate significance like dark blood sent blushing to the face from the heart's deep music. The rich colours seen by the mystic impel him to action. Our cosmic scheme must never remain static. It is not only a design, but a drama too, the quintessence of whose imagery is verbal music. The only purely unspatial and temporal art, that of music, must be added to, or rather inwoven with, our scheme of elements, not only in the sense of an immediate harmony and ever-springing dawn, but in wider rhythms of day and night, life and death, and the sun-cycle of the seasons, till, as fine architecture to the inward eye, the universe of earth, fire, air and water is felt thrusting itself up, second by second, hour by hour, aeon by aeon, which is its rhythmic nature and eternity quality, its music. For the space-time dimension is eternity, which is why it curves over, a sweeping rainbow arc. There is thus no final antagonism between philosophies of space and time, which are twin approaches to a more richly dimensional whole.'

(VII, 215)

These pieces, published in 1936, describe, far better than I could say it today, the *alpha* and *omega* of my own writings, and what they claim to reveal. At the heart of my other original work, *The Dynasty of Stowe* (VI), part of the mansion's North Front is imagined as dissolving to reveal the living persons of its past owners, and the personification of Stowe, again flowering from the structure, proceeds to speak its oracles in such paradoxes as we have been discussing.

But though such symbols are centres of considerable importance, they cease to be so the moment we forget their circles. Valuable though it may be to describe, or create, such revealing paradoxes, it is still finer to work up, as Shakespeare and Byron work up, the action-pose of a human drama into the musical building of some expanded artistic form. Ivory towers, as Tennyson wrote his *Palace of Art*, itself rich with these symbolic properties, to demonstrate, are a second-best, and may be a danger. They symbolize man's relation to eternity; but they do no more; they do not fuse his most pressing concerns, as does drama, with the eternal dimension.

Before approaching Pope's poem, I would call attention to three theorists of importance in our present context. One is, naturally, Lessing, whose *Laocoön* is the classic document on the interdependence and inter-relationship of the arts of space and time, and of the ways in which they can, or cannot, encroach on one another. Two scenes from Elizabethan drama make interesting dramatic footnotes, or forecastings, of Lessing's book. One is that remarkable dialogue between Hieronimo and the Painter occurring in the anonymous additions to *The Spanish Tragedy* (III, xii*a*); the other, the dialogue between Poet and Painter in *Timon of Athens* (I, i). Though they do not develop Lessing's thesis, these scenes serve to throw up, in sharp dramatic terms, the nature of his problem.

The next is Nietzsche's *The Birth of Tragedy*. Nietzsche sees drama, and indeed life in general, as composed of two powers, or principles. The first is the 'Dionysian': the dark origins of creation, numinous and mystic, energic, even violent, orgiastic, unmoral, of sound rather than sight, of 'the unconscious', as we should say. The other is the 'Apollonian': the created ideal, the vision in and beyond creation; conscious, intellectual, of daylight. The one is dynamic, the other, in comparison, static; the typifying art of the one is *music*, of the other *sculpture*. Though here Nietzsche is at pains to emphasize the importance of the Dionysian, his aim is the fusion of the two; and in his other great imaginative work, *Thus Spake Zarathustra*, he celebrates and defines the fusion in terms, recalling Pope's *Essay on Man*, of human psychology; in terms, we might say, of the human workshop.[1]

Our third theorist, unfortunately little known though a thinker of great importance, is the French aesthetic and dramatic theorist of the last century, François Delsarte, whose three basic principles were drawn from the study of ancient statuary. They are (i) opposition, (ii) sequence, and (iii) poise. 'Opposition' in statuary is normally apparent in a certain sympathy existing between the head and lower limbs, and countered by a torso tending differently. 'Sequence', being temporal, can in statuary, as opposed to dramatic art, be only suggested. In 'poise' these two principles are blended; and somehow this blend gives us a breath of eternal life.[2]

III

Such is our introduction to Pope's *Temple of Fame* (1711–1715). We shall proceed to show, though his favourite field is the far harder one of strict human delineation, yet that he has, in his one attempt at such symbolic writing, shown himself a master of it.

Pope's poetry, irrespective of its subject, holds just such a 'poise' as Delsarte has defined. In terms of the Delsartian trinity we can draw a rather useful contrast between the poetic styles of Milton and Pope. To use his own words from the preface to *Paradise Lost*, Milton's *forte* lies in 'the sense variously drawn out from one line to another'; it is, as my essay 'The Frozen Labyrinth' in *The Burning Oracle* argued, essentially narrative and winding, even music in *L'Allegro* being defined as a 'winding bout of linked sweetness long drawn out'. 'Sequence' clearly tends to dominate. But since literature is already and inevitably a temporal art, this is dangerous; and the danger is countered by weight of diction, solidification of image, and various other means, as it were, of weighting down, clogging, the forward progress; of putting on the brake. The result is control

[1] *Christ and Nietzsche*, v.

[2] I have in typescript a work *Symbol of Man* relating Delsarte's theories to photographs of the human form.

rather than balance. In Pope, however, we have a very clear sense of opposition and balance, as with the two halves of his regularly divided line-units and of the rhymed couplet itself. Each, line and couplet, is, in itself, a balanced unit. His verse paragraphs are also units, succeeding each other, as, pre-eminently, in *Eloisa to Abelard*, in alternate, balanced, pieces, like a graceful walk. Writing of Pope's use of variation, George Sherburn tells us that 'eighteenth-century art depended not on long crescendoes leading to orgiastic climaxes, but on balance and alternation of tone'.[1] In a temporal art sequence is anyway assured, and Pope shows no lack of smooth continuity. As a result, we have poise or grace, rather than control; and this is what we mean, or should mean, whenever we think or talk of peace. Writing of the happier, non-satiric, types of eighteenth-century poetry, Sherburn relates the moment of poetic release to a 'consciousness of being perfectly poised in life, perfectly at peace in its green pastures'.[2]

Pope's world shows a harmony as assured as, though less geometrical than, Dante's. His poetic philosophy rests on two basic principles as centre and circumference: (i) the secret impulses of nature within man, and (ii) the cosmic whole. Man is the centre, as in Dante's final vision. But Pope is far more humanist, Greek, Renaissance, in emphasis. Man is allowed greater status as a dynamic unit. How is Pope to be placed in our present context?

We need not, I think, be surprised to find that, in the one poem in which he so engages himself throughout, published at the height of his interest in painting, he should have left us a handling and grouping of symbolisms surpassed by none of the various treatments which we have passed in review. *The Temple of Fame* compactly includes all the effects in question, neatly grouped, inter-related with each other, given exact place in a rational and time-honoured scheme, and finally pointed to ethic: that is, they are valued. I am not arguing that Pope's peculiar excellence in this province proves him an abler poet than those who have achieved less in it. But I do assert that *The Temple of Fame* serves to compact and crown our discussion.

Here are some preliminary points. *The Temple of Fame* contains some of our very finest realizations of the action-pose, together

[1] *Selections from Alexander Pope*, New York (1929); Int., xxxiii.

[2] *Selections*, xxxvi. F. R. Leavis in *Revaluation* (1936) at one point uses the word 'poise' to characterize Pope's artistry.

with perhaps our finest example of a living architecture. The Greek and Medieval may be supposed as to this extent balanced. Though the architecture is rather classic than Gothic, the Gothic is included; and the whole design, though humanist in content, remains medieval in conception, being directly derived from Chaucer's *Hous of Fame*, to which, however, its main excellences owe nothing. But it is romantic too: we have not only a sacred structure, but a structure placed on the summit of a mountain; and though in this Pope is following a medieval tradition, for you find the same in Chaucer and the throne of Fortune in *Timon of Athens* (I, i, 65), Pope's mountain is very much more exciting in the romantic manner. So much for the major substances. In detail, *The Temple of Fame* avoids all the limitations and weaknesses, intentional or unintentional, that are liable to attend such impressions. Though many of the Miltonic elements are included, there is no trace of stiffness in use of artefacts, gems, or bejewelled mounts; nor any undertone of decadence, laziness or premature solutions, as, variously, in the intentional impressions of artificiality to which C. S. Lewis has drawn our attention [1] in Spenser's 'Bower of Bliss', or those of Tennyson's *Palace of Art*, Browning's *The Statue and the Bust*, or Yeats' *Sailing to Byzantium*; nor any of that unintended facility in use of the dome or other architectures which might be a charge levelled at the Romantics in general. Our symbols are as highly charged as those in *Kubla Khan*, Keats' *Grecian Urn*, or *Abt Vogler*. The exploitation of sounds, both dulcet and jarring, challenges comparison with Milton and Wordsworth (e.g. in his ode *On the Power of Sound*). Human energies are included at every instant and the major statement as deeply relevant to world affairs as that of *The Iron Christ*. There is a sense of the transcendent as surely as at the conclusion to *The Winter's Tale*, in Byron's statue poetry, and *Abt Vogler*. But it is not exactly mystical, nor metaphysical; the abstruse metaphysics of Donne and Eliot are avoided, though much of their basic thought subsumed. There is throughout a stern realism. Though presented in full power and authority, the symbols are deliberately valued. The Goddess of Fame is exactly what the title implies; no more, and no less. 'Fame' is a great concept, piercing the eternal dimension; but the Goddess remains enigmatic, sometimes, it is true, felt as the personification of divine justice, but sometimes shown as irresponsible.

There is, however, no uncertainty in the moral. Our symbolisms

[1] *The Allegory of Love*, VII, 324–9.

are related to ethic, to virtue; but not to any static or theoretic virtue; the great strivings of man's past are given concrete and individual embodiment and finally judged, if not by the Goddess, by the poet. The conclusion witnesses a selfless humility. The poem's manner itself possesses the reserve Lessing noted as a characteristic of ancient sculpture, not only in descriptions of the action-pose, but in its own technique, its every moment of poetic poise. Spatial and temporal conceptions and substances intermix, as in Keats, only with a far greater relevance to human actuality, without becoming fluid, or ceasing to be themselves. There is a supervening harmony, as in Dante, but with all human energies and rights preserved. The whole is lucid, coherent and objective. A child could understand it.

We next offer a brief commentary. The poet, vaguely located 'betwixt earth, seas and skies', surveys 'the whole creation' in panorama:

In air self-balanc'd hung the globe below,
Where mountains rise and circling oceans flow;
Here naked rocks, and empty wastes were seen,
There tow'ry cities, and the forests green:
Here sailing ships delight the wand'ring eyes:
There trees, and intermingled temples rise.

(13)

He is startled by a strange sound, like 'broken thunders' or the murmuring of ocean—the sounds throughout are important—and suddenly sees a 'glorious pile' piercing the clouds:

High on a rock of Ice the structure lay,
Steep its ascent, and slipp'ry was the way;
The wond'rous rock like Parian marble shone,
And seem'd, to distant sight, of solid stone.

(27)

On it he could see names inscribed; most were obliterated by time, and some appeared only to dissolve. Some were worn or melted by storm or sun, these corresponding precisely to the twin dangers of hostility and excessive adulation, but others survive despite all trials:

Yet part no injuries of heav'n could feel,
Like crystal faithful to the graving steel:
The rock's high summit, in the temple's shade,
Nor heat could melt, nor beating storm invade.

Their names inscrib'd unnumber'd ages past
From time's first birth, with time itself shall last;
These ever new, nor subject to decays,
Spread, and grow brighter with the length of days.

(45)

It is a spiritual mount, resembling in its impressions of ice certain favourite poetic intuitions of Coleridge, especially his 'sunny pleasure-dome with caves of ice' in *Kubla Khan*:

So Zembla's rocks (the beauteous work of frost)
Rise white in air, and glitter o'er the coast;
Pale suns, unfelt, at distance roll away,
And on th' impassive ice the lightnings play;
Eternal snows the growing mass supply,
Till the bright mountains prop th' incumbent sky:
As Atlas fix'd, each hoary pile appears,
The gather'd winter of a thousand years.

(53)

The word 'eternal' is important, and it recurs. On this white mountain-rock stands the Temple of Fame, 'stupendous', 'not rear'd by mortal hands' (62), and surpassing the finest creations of Babylon, Greece, or Rome.

The 'dome', a word which sometimes means no more than house (Latin, *domus*), is square, with four 'faces', each different, and with four brazen gates (65–7). The Western front is of Greek architecture:

Westward, a sumptuous frontispiece appear'd,
On Doric pillars of white marble rear'd,
Crown'd with an architrave of antique mold,
And sculpture rising on the roughen'd gold.

(75)

Our dominant visual impressions throughout are of white and gold, signifying a rich spirituality, or purity. On this front are sculptured mythical heroes: Theseus, Perseus, Hercules. The sculpturings, with a subtle enjoyment of artistic mingling, or interplay, show music functioning as a creative force, as trees 'start from their roots' to Orpheus' art and Amphion's 'creating lyre' is seen making Thebes to rise (79–88). The impressions are of vivid, immediate, up-springing vitality. It is all happening while we watch, with a kinship to that peculiar immediacy that so characterizes Goethe's poetry. Here is Thebes, flowering to, and from, music:

There might you see the length'ning spires ascend,
The domes swell up, the wid'ning arches bend,
The growing tow'rs, like exhalations rise,
And the huge columns heave into the skies.

(89)

A lovely description recalling our other buildings to music, in Milton, Coleridge, Browning, Keats, and O'Shaughnessy. The *still sculpture* itself catches the *action* of *architecture* springing from *music*, and all this is reported in *poetry*: we could scarcely have a more complex, and yet so lucid, compacting of our various themes.

The Eastern front is more gorgeous, 'flaming' with diamonds and 'barbaric gold', like certain spectacular pieces of *Paradise Lost* (III, 505–8; V, 753–63). On it we have Ninus the Assyrian, Cyrus of Persia, the 'royal Magi' in 'long robes', while, with a finely characterizing action, 'Grave Zoroaster waves the circling wand' (93–8). There are Chaldeans in white, and Brahmans in their forests, adepts at magic, at raising the dead, men who

Made visionary fabrics round them rise,
And airy spectres skim before their eyes.

(103)

But, with a reminder typical of Pope's approach, we are told that Confucius stands apart, 'superior and alone', being rated above the rest in view of his more 'useful science' of ethical teaching (107–8). The Southern front, which is Egyptian, shows priests in gilded niches, learned in geometry and astronomy. Here is a good miniature:

High on his car Sesostris struck my view,
Whom scepter'd slaves in golden harness drew:
His hands a bow and pointed javelin hold;
His giant limbs are arm'd in scales of gold.

(113)

Every time you feel the action of the people depicted, without forgetting that it *is* depicted. The poetry gets the essence of each action-pose, as such.

On the North, there is Gothic art 'o'erwrought with ornaments of barb'rous pride' (120). We have Zamolxis, student of immortality, with 'erected eyes' (123), and Odin shown falling into one of his 'trances' (124): every detail is alive and active, yet never is the picture forgotten. There are 'Runic characters' (122), grim Scythians on iron blood-smeared columns, Druids and Bards, and many more of what Pope, with his hatred of militarism, calls 'doubtful fame' (129). The wall is interesting:

> *The wall in lustre and effect like Glass,*
> *Which o'er each object casting various dyes,*
> *Enlarges some, and others multiplies:*
> *Nor void of emblem was the mystic wall,*
> *For thus romantic Fame increases all.*
>
> (132)

The wall is 'mystic'; its supernatural powers are not doubted, and yet Fame is called 'romantic', because it sometimes romanticizes. Notice how subtly our sense-impressions and various solids are impregnated with exact meaning.

The living structure—it functions as a live thing—opens to reveal its interior:

> *The Temple shakes, the sounding gates unfold,*
> *Wide vaults appear, and roofs of fretted gold:*
> *Rais'd on a thousand pillars, wreath'd around*
> *With laurel-foliage, and with eagles crown'd:*
> *Of bright transparent beryl were the walls,*
> *The friezes gold, and gold the capitals:*
> *As heav'n with stars, the roof with jewels glows,*
> *And ever-living lamps depend in rows.*
>
> (137)

The roof is a sort of heaven, and the lamps 'ever-living'. Inside, we find sculptures of 'sage Historians in white garments' who have conquered time:

> *Grav'd o'er their seats the form of Time was found,*
> *His scythe revers'd, and both his pinions bound.*
>
> (147)

We have Alexander throned, with feet on subject sceptres and tiaras; and Caesar, master of the world and himself, 'unmoved' and 'superior' (157). But most important, we are told, the strong ethical emphasis persisting, are the more selfless heroes, Epaminondas, Timoleon, Scipio, and Aurelius of 'unbounded virtue'. The valuation is at once heroic and Christian, with particular honour to 'those of less noisy, and less guilty Fame' who silently serve virtue; and so we pass to 'the godlike Socrates', Phocion, Agis, Cato and Brutus (159–77).

We have next some beautiful studies of great writers, placed on pillars arranged in a *circle* round the Temple's centre, nearest, as Pope's note tells us, to the throne of Fame. 'Mighty Homer' is set high on a throne of 'eternal Adamant' (183), solidity being exactly used to signify spiritual with lasting fame. Our impressions are here to be peculiarly rich, with a fine sense, not merely of action, but of inward, spiritualized, qualities pictorially and dramatically expressed, as in the second line of an earlier couplet of remarkable power:

Heroes in animated marble frown,
And Legislators seem to think in stone.

(73)

So now, of Homer:

Father of verse! in holy fillets drest,
His silver beard wav'd gently o'er his breast.

(184)

True, Homer is not so deeply spiritualized as some others, since his work is mainly on the more simple, heroic, level: so, 'Tho' blind, a boldness in his looks appears' (186). As a great poet, he is venerable, but his themes are violent:

The wars of Troy were round the Pillar seen:
Here fierce Tydides wounds the Cyprian Queen;
Here Hector glorious from Patroclus' fall,
Here dragg'd in triumph round the Trojan wall,
Motion and life did ev'ry part inspire,
Bold was the work, and prov'd the master's fire.

(188)

'Motion and life': the lines apply both to the Homeric poetry and to its visual presentation. The actions are left rather vague since Pope remains distrustful of militaristic emotions. He wants the art without any close-up of its subject. When we come to Virgil we find less disparity between art's serenity and warlike action—Pope is, one feels, troubled by this paradox—and we are aware of a new depth, a dignity different in kind, directly related to the poet's artistry. He is found in a shrine 'of purest gold' showing exquisite finish, 'with patient touches of unweary'd art':

The Mantuan there in sober triumph sate,
Compos'd his posture, and his look sedate;
On Homer still he fix'd a rev'rend eye,
Great without pride, in modest majesty.
In living sculpture on the sides were spread
The Latian Wars, and haughty Turnus dead . . .

Again, the brutality of war is slurred. As for the 'living sculpture', that is our reiterated emphasis, rising to a climax in the succeeding lines, wherein Pindar is felt with an extraordinarily interesting distinction from the other figures exactly relevant to Nietzsche's thesis in *The Birth of Tragedy*, as *melting into his own music*:

Four swans sustain a car of silver bright,
With heads advanc'd, and pinions stretch'd for flight:
Here, like some furious prophet, Pindar rode,
And seem'd to labour with th' inspiring God.
Across the harp a careless hand he flings,
And boldly sinks into the sounding strings.
The figur'd games of Greece the column grace,
Neptune and Jove survey the rapid race.
The youths hang o'er their chariots as they run;
The fiery steeds seem starting from the stone;
The champions in distorted postures threat;
And all appear'd irregularly great.

This passage is of considerable importance. Nietzsche distinguishes the dithyramb and lyric, and to this *genre* Pindar's poetry preeminently belongs, from epic, in that the lyrist is identified with the music, is one with the Dionysian 'I am', whereas the epic poet composes more externally, is more objective.[1] Now this identification with the music is also the theme of Browning's *Abt Vogler*, where the artist both creates and *is* the music, for a while; it is also what Eliot means by 'music heard so deeply that it is not heard at all' and 'you are the music while the music lasts'.[2] Pindar, the prototype of such

[1] *The Birth of Tragedy*, V, VI.

[2] *The Dry Salvages*, V.

art, is, with exact import, shown accordingly as melting into his music; letting, with a grand abandon, the music speak through him, as subject. His theme is, like Homer's, physical action, but there is a difference. Athletics replace war, and a strong representation is the more readily allowed. We may think that Lessing's principle, drawn from his study of the *Laocoön* group and other ancient works, on the importance of avoiding the moment of physical violence, is here ignored. But observe that all Pope's other miniatures show a fine reserve; the power of Pindar exists in his careless, yet bold, *relaxation*. Violence is, however, in place for his 'champions', since neither the actual bloodshed of war nor the spiritual connotations of art are involved. The very violence ('distorted') suggests a deliberated and controlled presentation to give a sculptural equivalent to the subject: it is the business of such contestants, as it is not the business of a Laocoön, to look like that. Such are the exactitudes characterizing Pope's impressions.

With Aristotle, the philosopher, there are naturally no such complexities:

Here in a shrine that cast a dazzling light,
Sate fix'd in thought the mighty Stagirite;
His sacred head a radiant Zodiac crown'd,
And various Animals his sides surround;
His piercing eyes, erect, appear to view
Superior worlds, and look all Nature through.

(232)

And we have a beautiful example of the pure, suggestive, action-pose, in description of Cicero:

Gath'ring his flowing robe, he seem'd to stand
In act to speak, and graceful stretch'd his hand.

(240)

A positive treasure-store of noble sculptures exists in this richly compacted poem.

These plastic yet ever-living figures are being used for a transcendent purpose as surely as the statue of Hermione in Shakespeare, or the snapshot actions on Keats' Grecian urn; they serve to realize an intuition of eternal validity in the great persons concerned. The Temple is itself a spiritual temple, a kind of temple of eternity, to be equated with other such throughout poetic symbolism, though never was there a finer presentation. The descriptions are loaded with impressions of gold and rich gems set against the prevailing whiteness, and the architectures are felt as living. The main fabrics resemble those of the magicians who, as we have seen, 'made visionary fabrics round them rise' (103); and when we hear that 'six pompous columns o'er the rest aspire' (179), the purposeful, living impact of 'aspire' is organic. The specifically architectural descriptions culminate in a circular, or spherical, impressionism, rising to a noble climax:

These massy columns in a circle rise,
O'er which a pompous dome invades the skies:
Scarce to the top I stretch'd my aching sight,
So large it spread, and swell'd to such a height.
Full in the midst proud Fame's imperial seat,
With jewels blaz'd, magnificently great;
The vivid em'ralds there revive the eye,
The flaming rubies shew their sanguine dye,
Bright azure rays from lively sapphyrs stream,
And lucid amber casts a golden gleam.
With various-colour'd light the pavement shone,
And all on fire appear'd the glowing throne;
The dome's high arch reflects the mingled blaze,
And forms a rainbow of alternate rays.
When on the Goddess first I cast my sight,
Scarce seem'd her stature of a cubit's height;
But swell'd to larger size, the more I gaz'd,
Till to the roof her tow'ring front she rais'd.
With her, the Temple ev'ry moment grew,
And ampler Vista's open'd to my view:
Upward the columns shoot, the roofs ascend,
And arches widen, and long aisles extend.
Such was her form as ancient bards have told,
Wings raise her arms, and wings her feet infold;
A thousand busy tongues the Goddess bears,
And thousand open eyes, and thousand list'ning ears.
Beneath, in order rang'd, the tuneful Nine
(Her virgin handmaids) still attend the shrine:
With eyes on Fame for ever fix'd, they sing;
For Fame they raise the voice, and tune the string;

With time's first birth began the heav'nly lays,
And last, eternal, thro' the length of days.

(244)

As in Byron's description of St. Peter's, the building's size is conditioned by the onlooker's gathering assimilation. It is not merely an object, but an experience, and the experience involves effort as the 'aching sight' pierces upward. The temple is more mystical, more symbolical, than Byron's St. Peter's, and it is vividly alive. We must not for one instant forget that this is the Temple of Fame, and that she is *exactly what her name implies*. So the gems and colours are all 'lively' and shown in ceaseless interplay, as though the richly accumulated values of the human tradition across the centuries were always both borrowing from and lending each other new splendours of meaning. It is, you see, the creative process and eternal purpose behind these rich and inter-active accomplishments of great men that the poet's artistry expresses. That is why the Temple grows moment by moment larger as subsequent insight gradually, as, for example, with the reputation of a Shakespeare, clarifies, and significance matures. Its expansion is both vertical and horizontal ('Upward . . . extend'), both eternity and time being under survey. The Goddess herself is visualized in phrases reminiscent of Biblical prophecy. She is mistress of a multitude of human tongues, eyes, ears; all the creative activity and sense-impressions of mankind are her implements; almost she is That for which man's consciousness exists. In especial, the arts, or Muses, serve her in interpreting, ratifying, and perpetuating, indeed all but creating, the values in question. Such 'Fame' may be called a supreme value for which other lesser values exist; it was born at time's origin, but its life is 'eternal'. See how our living and mainly spherical architecture generates itself while we watch—it is all dramatic, in the ever-present 'now' of dramatic art—and how the whole is crowned by song and music; while the concluding impact of the word 'eternal' supervenes on, or rather flowers from, a ceaseless activity, rather like the vivid interplay of swirling, dance-like action and supervening harmony throughout Dante's *Paradiso*.

Such is the wealth of meaning smoothly housed in Pope's most elaborate use of this symbolism. We have here a good example of what Byron meant by calling Pope's a 'poetry without fault' (p. 130 below).

Here the poem could have ended, and some of us might wish that it had. But this is not Pope's way: for one thing, he does not base his art on the climax, his favourite technique being undulatory; [1] for another, he is not quite content with his goddess, great though she be. Even though she be all but equated with eternity, it is only his own intuition of the eternal. Besides, can we trust in anything called Fame as wholly reliable? And if we could, would this be enough? Are there not other, more purely ethical, compulsions to be watched? Is this goddess *moral*?

She is enigmatic. 'All the nations' come at the sound of her doom-like 'trumpet' (277–8), 'millions' of suppliants attending of every conceivable variety:

Their pleas were diff'rent, their request the same:
For good and bad alike are fond of Fame.

(292)

We find her disgracing some and honouring others: 'unlike successes equal merits found' (295). The line is ambiguous: has she, or has she not, her own good reasons for her decisions? There is a certain doubt.

Thus her blind sister, fickle Fortune, reigns,
And, undiscerning, scatters crowns and chains.

(296)

That seems clear enough, but it is not the whole truth.

After all, she has so far been shown as an able goddess, with our historic figures well ordered and grouped. Moreover, she is next shown ratifying the finest values. When the learned come pale with study to ask her reward, her reception is described in a noble passage introduced, again, by the authoritative word 'eternal', and rich with circular impressions and a subtle use of sound and smell:

The Goddess heard, and bade the Muses raise
The golden Trumpet of eternal Praise:
From pole to pole the winds diffuse the sound,
That fills the circuit of the world around;
Not all at once, as thunder breaks the cloud;
The notes at first were rather sweet than loud . . .

(306)

[1] See p. 92 above: and also Geoffrey Tillotson's section, 'Design'.

Though at first the choice few alone recognize the merit in question, the power grows, the notes get stronger:

By just degrees they ev'ry moment rise,
Fill the wide earth, and gain upon the skies.
At ev'ry breath were balmy odours shed,
Which still grew sweeter as they wider spread;
Less fragrant scents th' unfolding rose exhales,
Or spices breathing in Arabian gales.

(312)

The truly virtuous are likewise honoured:

Next these the good and just, an awful train,
Thus on their knees address the sacred fane.
'Since living virtue is with envy curs'd,
And the best men are treated like the worst,
Do thou, just Goddess, call our merits forth,
And give each deed th' exact intrinsic worth.'

(318)

That is exactly how we want her, as Goddess of true Fame, or valuation, to function. But she does not always do so. Another virtuous band appears, only to have their claims ruined by slander:

But straight the direful Trump of Slander sounds;
Thro' the big dome the doubling thunder bounds;
Loud as the burst of cannon rends the skies,
The dire report thro' ev'ry region flies,
In ev'ry ear incessant rumours rung,
And gath'ring scandals grew on ev'ry tongue.
From the black trumpet's rusty concave broke
Sulphureous flames, and clouds of rolling smoke:
The pois'nous vapour blots the purple skies,
And withers all before it as it flies.

(332)

Again, a fine exploitation of sound. But we may, indeed, wonder why the Goddess allows such slanders to obscure true merit, since she functions normally as a just arbiter, never more so than when she disappoints the expectations of great conquerors, crowned and armed, proud and defiant, men who for fame 'swam to empire thro' the purple flood' (347), and expect renown:

'Ambitious fools!' (the Queen reply'd, and frown'd)
'Be all your acts in dark oblivion drown'd;
There sleep forgot, with mighty tyrants gone,
Your statues moulder'd, and your names unknown!'
A sudden cloud straight snatch'd them from my sight,
And each majestic phantom sunk in night.

(350)

What they did *seemed* to be virtue (349), and they *are* majestic (355). We watch Pope making an advance beyond the heroic tradition; while using its terms, he is redirecting it. Fact is falsified, since great conquerors *have* been remembered, but he is really out to define a result that should be, not only what is. His whole poem is, as it were, a search for just fame, for eternal virtue. Therefore those who were indifferent to fame and followed virtue for its own sake are greeted by a 'trembling music' that spreads 'triumphant',

So soft, tho' high, so loud, and yet so clear,
Ev'n list'ning Angels lean'd from heav'n to hear.

(374)

Here, again, the Goddess fulfils our expectations, functioning as an eternal rather than as a temporal arbitress.

But we are next again surprised to find her allowing the claims of certain fashionable young men, who, unsuccessful in love, yet wish to have the reputation of amorous conquest; and their claim is allowed, even at the expense of the ladies' honour (378–93). There appears to be some justice at work here, since another group, 'unlearn'd in arts to please' (396), is peremptorily dismissed. Traitors certainly get their deserts:

Last, those who boast of mighty mischiefs done,
Enslave their country, or usurp a throne;
Or who their glory's dire foundation lay'd
On Sov'reigns ruin'd, or on friends betray'd;
Calm, thinking villains, whom no faith could fix,
Of crooked counsels and dark politics;
Of these a gloomy tribe surround the throne,
And beg to make th' immortal treasons known.
The trumpet roars, long flaky flames expire
With sparks, that seem'd to set the world on fire.

At the dread sound, pale mortals stood aghast,
And startled nature trembled with the blast.

(406)

Again we are satisfied.

As though to attempt a clarification, our scene, following Chaucer (III, 822 ff.), shifts from the Temple of Fame to another temple, or centre, of Rumour. It is called

a structure fair
Its site uncertain, if in earth or air.

(420)

The 'mansion' whirls round 'with rapid motion' (422), and there is continual noise. This is a receptacle, a magnet, drawing all *sounds* whatsoever to itself from the earth:

Nor ever silence, rest, or peace is here.

(435)

The passage grows metaphysical, out of all proportion to the subject. Pope was apparently attracted by an earlier passage of Chaucer's poem (II, 257–314) on sound, and works it in here. Just as a stone dropped in water makes widening and ever-widening circles, so sound, we are told, impresses itself on air:

Thus ev'ry voice and sound, when first they break,
On neighb'ring air a soft impression make;
Another ambient circle then they move;
That, in its turn, impels the next above;
Thro' undulating air the sounds are sent,
And spread o'er all the fluid element.

(442)

The 'soft impression' suggests Rudolf Steiner's theory that sounds actually carve corresponding shapes, or figures, in the air. We are faced by an interesting attempt to feel sound spatially; it functions in circular, spatial, waves. The passage accordingly falls neatly into place for our general purpose.

As for Rumour, the thoughts are fairly obvious, and not unlike the Shakespearian exposition in the Induction of 2 *Henry IV*. A list of falsities is presented, with their snowball tendency to grow worse duly noted. False news flies fast, spreading like fire. Such lies reach the home of Rumour, who returns them to earth when perfected. And all this appears to be allowed, even controlled, by Fame:

Fame sits aloft, and points them out their course,
Their date determines, and prescribes their force.

(483)

'Date' means their date of expiry. Some soon die. Others—Pope may be thinking of the reputation of poets—'wane and wax alternate like the moon' (486). Sometimes you see a lie and truth 'contending' for passage, both finally going forth 'inseparable' or 'for ever join'd' (494–5); an exquisite penetration of what does, in fact, often happen, especially with the reputations of men of genius.

Our conclusion is spoken in the poet's own person. He is warned that the favour of Fame is, after all, a vain quest:

How vain that second life in others' breath.

(505)

It can be a mad pursuit, attended by much disquiet, much hostility. The final passage makes a perfect statement:

Nor Fame I slight, nor for her favours call;
She comes unlook'd for, if she comes at all.
But if the purchase costs so dear a price,
As soothing Folly, or exalting Vice:
Oh! if the Muse must flatter lawless sway,
And follow still where fortune leads the way;
Or if no basis bear my rising name,
But the fall'n ruin of another's fame;
Then teach me, heav'n! to scorn the guilty bays,
Drive from my breast that wretched lust of praise,
Unblemish'd let me live, or die unknown;
Oh grant an honest fame, or grant me none!

(513)

Our conclusions serves, if not to elucidate, certainly to crown, our earlier ambiguities.

The goddess Fame appears to fulfil incompatible functions. She is both (i) a goddess of eternal valuation ratifying the true and denouncing the false, and (ii) a personification of the random action of fame, or rumour, on earth.[1] Perhaps the two may be assimilated under the heading of 'realism', since, in actual experience, good name and lasting preservation is, on the whole, a resultant and an assessment of one's actions, though we are also aware of many injustices. We can say that Pope, working in a humanist tradition, and building on Chaucer, starts to write an allegorical poem on Fame; and in the process, not only does his symbolism outdistance Chaucer's, since the peculiar excellences which we have noticed, except for the passage on sound, are not in Chaucer, but even where he to some extent follows, as he does, the earlier master in delineation of the Goddess and her actions, his thinking adds a new intensity to the enigma which she presents as symbol simultaneously of divine authority and the perversities of fortune. The whole reflects Pope's own survey, from a personal view, and the conclusion tidies everything, with its assertion of righteousness and humility as the only certainty. If the Goddess is ambiguous, the moral of the poem is not.

The poem's first half, concluding with the great temple description, is concerned with what is known from the past, and it would seem that the Goddess is, so far, considered a divine dispenser of justice. Her actual accomplishments are before us: Homer and Aristotle are, in fact, remembered. But the poet may next be felt wondering if she is always just. Have other good and great men been either forgotten or slandered? You cannot be sure. He is, perhaps, thinking now of himself and of the present, or future, and in so thinking deliberately discusses the Goddess' apparent irresponsibility. There is always, in these matters, a vast difference between past records and present anxieties, as with the easy acceptance of destructive forces as part of God's scheme, provided it all be an old story, but the far harder matter of acceptance for ourselves, here and now. That is another way of looking at our problem.

There is yet a third, perhaps the most important of all. Even if Pope's Goddess is regarded as only in part reliable, that does not mean that his greater passages are less meaningful, nor any the less symbols of the eternal. The fame which interests Pope is poetic fame; the Temple's centre, with its poets and philosophers, makes that abundantly clear. Now poetry and philosophy are themselves techniques of traffic with the eternal, and any fame so won is necessarily a fame close to eternal status. We have, accordingly, a clustered

[1] Tillotson observes 'an incompletely stated connection between the two temples, that of Fame and that of Rumour', 'Design', 55.

association of poetry, fame and eternity. But, and even if this be an expansion of Pope's explicit meaning, it most certainly touches the *reasons* lying beneath his surface, Pope may, without any slighting of its importance, yet be felt as unwilling to give this 'cluster' unqualified homage. Why? Because eternal insight is not enough. *Kubla Khan* had that, and so has Keats' *Grecian Urn*; but do either make any contact with morality? Confucius' teaching was considered as more important than miracle and magic (107). Life to Pope, as to Byron, takes precedence over art, even though that very precedence becomes again art's subject. 'Eternity' no doubt covers everything, but symbols of it, however exquisite, are not enough. Pope is with Shakespeare and Byron as poets of actual human affairs who only occasionally indulge in such symbolisms; and even more than they, he is, as Byron urged, a poet of morality. That is why he was impelled from the depths to leave his goddess and her attendant symbolisms ambiguous.

After all, we have watched certain of the virtuous honoured precisely because they never looked for fame (366). Pope finally realizes that 'She comes unlook'd for if she comes at all' (514). Fame is one of those things that you may have, in New Testament phrase, to lose in order to find. In the poem's latter parts Pope is writing from a new viewpoint, taking his stand within the centre of his own personal engagements; it is rather like the contrast of Epistles II and III with Epistle I in the *Essay on Man*. That his noble conclusion had a very deep meaning for himself may be hinted by a biographical reminder. Poetic fame was with him a burning desire, and he knew the attendant temptations, and the dangers of spiritual pride. More, he built himself a little 'temple': his famous grotto. In this period, the great houses, grounds, statues and grottoes of noblemen were extensions of the personalities, as indeed are all possessions, of their owners. They were works of personal pride, of flamboyance. 'Vanity', wrote Dr. Johnson in his Life of Pope—and by 'vanity' he would have meant something like 'showiness'—'produced a grotto where necessity enforced a passage.' Bonamy Dobrée comments:

'Well, there may have been a touch of vanity at the beginning, but the celebrated grotto was a delirious fantasy in which Pope let himself go; for year after year it was his great toy, his unfailing release, and he kept on improving and enlarging it, lining the walls with different kinds of stone and crystals, ores and corals, arranging mirrors to enhance the effect, placing a thin alabaster lamp to strengthen the glooms, and contriving the most cunning waterworks, little cascades and rills, which twisting about made gurgles and splashes, and "a little dripping murmur".'

(*Alexander Pope*, v, 70)

There you have his own, personal, little temple; his little temple of fame. It was, if you like, his 'ivory tower', and, like all ivory towers, it had its dangers. The conclusion to *The Temple of Fame* acknowledges the danger: that is all.

To return to our symbolisms. We point to: (i) the exquisite miniatures of sculptured action, which are at once action, sculpture and poetry; (ii) the mountain-based temple with its living architecture and music; (iii) the use of sounds, dulcet or harsh, the peculiar preserve of Milton and Wordsworth, together with an exciting attempt, following Chaucer, to give sound a spatial definition. All these, and other related, effects are exactly ordered with details meticulously fitted to the general meanings, and all are, through the Goddess's ambiguity and the poem's conclusion, pointed beyond themselves and honestly placed, as far as the poet's personal experience at this early period could place them, in direct relation to the duties of actual life. Their relevance should be clear. From the start the 'dome' was Pope's symbol for the perfect poetic 'whole' (*Essay on Criticism*, 247–52; for other domes, see pp. 25, 33, 60, 95–6, 101). It, and architecture in general, may, here and elsewhere, be felt as balanced against 'nature' as is the great 'whole' of the *Essay on Man*, which all such structures symbolize.

I do not contend that this is Pope's greatest poem, nor that all our poets are entering a competition with regard to this particular province of their art. But I do contend that this is a province of central importance, and that Pope has mastered it with a peculiar felicity and exactitude. Each poet in turn has his own excellences unmatched elsewhere; but if we want, within a single poem, not merely a peculiarly fine poetic handling of 'the beauteous works of peace',[1] but a deliberate use of them as symbols of profound metaphysical importance, together with a grouping and compacting of such, and other, basic symbolisms in just relationship to each other and to wider issues, we shall find that in Pope's *Temple of Fame*, and there alone.

[1] *Windsor Forest*, 378.

IV

THE BOOK OF LIFE:

On Byron's Adulation of Pope

IV. THE BOOK OF LIFE

In this section I quote from Byron's *Letters and Journals* (LJ), edited by R. E. Prothero (Lord Ernle); and from *Byron: A Self-Portrait* (SP), edited by Peter Quennell. For the two lengthy sections which I call here and elsewhere the '*Blackwood's* Defence' and the 'Bowles Controversy', see pp. 131, 137 below.

I

In the preceding essays I have tried to do justice to the total meaning of Pope's poetry. His doctrinal challenge has hitherto been, in the main, resisted, not by open opposition, but by the far subtler and more effective means of pretending that it does not exist. Great poetry offers to distend our minds, but since few appear willing to risk 'the awful daring of a moment's surrender' which it asks of us, some form of defence mechanism is generally set up to avoid labour or embarrassment. Hence arises the tendency to reduce poetry to an appreciation of its manner, according it a purely technical, at the best a verbal, response, while ignoring those 'thousand charms' on which Pope himself, in his *Essay on Criticism*, so strongly insisted (pp. 42, 136); or we find scholars dissolving the various art-forms into their supposed 'sources' and crediting first the author, and next the art itself, with no more than an inorganic residue; or, again, as a last resort, the poetry is ignored and replaced by a concentration, generally to his severe disadvantage, on the poet's life. All this has happened to Pope. While such methods persist, the voice of poetry remains muffled; and when at last it is allowed to speak, the first reaction is likely to be one of incredulity or annoyance.

Nevertheless, the attempt must be made. Nor is our own attempt the first, since the gist of the argument has already been stated by a great man in a number of passages which together constitute a landmark in literary criticism; and anyone inclined to question the claims I have been making for Pope's poetic doctrine should consider the yet greater claims made for it by Lord Byron. There is a development, or tradition, still in process of formulation and reformulation, of which the first three figures are Shakespeare, Pope, and Byron; and the closer the attention which we give to them, both in themselves and in their inter-relationship, the more clearly shall we understand where we are today. We shall now discuss what Byron had to say of Pope, and also try to discover why it fell to him, alone among the great critics of our literature, to say it.

We have seen how Pope appears to preserve intact the quintessence of New Testament teaching whilst simultaneously re-establishing and consolidating a tradition of human powers and politics, at once classical and aristocratic, sinking its foundations to the ancient world; and in so doing he makes a statement of imperishable worth to Renaissance man. Now Byron, writing after a period of more revolution, including the French Revolution and the literary revolution inaugurated by Wordsworth and Coleridge, reasserted the values for which Pope stood. But his stage was far wider. In both his life and his poetry he reflected the European soul, the world-soul; and faced, as we are faced today, by a tumultuous anarchy of powers and passions, he rejected the theories of romanticism whilst looking back to Pope as an ideal and an exemplar; for there lay, in his view, the magic key. The scale was small, but it was the real thing. Though he himself in certain moods deplored his own concessions to romanticism, we can nevertheless regard his diction and style as a flowering from that same soil of traditional nobility that we recognize in the words of Pope. There is the same verbal solidity and rondure, the same surface lustre witnessing the vigour and the virtue within, the same incorporation of heroic energies and values, together with the same interpenetration of these with themes of liberalism, Christian ethic, civic righteousness, and all that constitutes, in general, the great 'campaign of peace' (p. 13 above). In both poets, as the message matures, the reliance on a poetic diction decreases; the diction has been dissolved into the message. Byron's problem was, briefly, Pope's. Political disruption he knew to be inevitable, and in part good; but in poetry, whose proper function he took to be the safeguard of those powers through which alone a new harmonization might be glimpsed, he was uncompromising in his reiterated assertion that the more individualistic extravagances of his day were pointing to disaster.

His admiration of Dryden and Pope, but especially of Pope, was clear from the start. Both *English Bards and Scotch Reviewers* (1809–11) and *Hints from Horace* (1811) show affinities of conception and treatment to the work of Pope: their tone is 'Augustan'.

English Bards and Scotch Reviewers is a remarkable achievement for a young poet. Within its light summary and critical review of current poetry, Crabbe alone, 'though nature's sternest painter, yet the best' (858), receives unqualified approval. Scott is both castigated and admired, being urged to leave absurd romances for subjects worthier of his genius (153–88, 911–48). Southey, Wordsworth and Coleridge get a series of knocks. Southey's prolific output in narrative is contrasted with the past, when one expected an epic once in a thousand years (189–234); Wordsworth, a 'dull disciple' of Southey, is called a 'mild apostate from poetic rule' (235–54); and 'gentle' Coleridge, 'the bard who soars to elegize an ass' (255–64). In contrast, honours are paid to Homer and Virgil (189–98), Shakespeare (592), Milton (187), 'great Dryden' (113, 187), Pope's 'pure strain' (109, 187), and also Massinger (592), Otway (115, 592), Congreve (115) and Sheridan (580–5). Shakespearian quotations are, as elsewhere in Byron, embedded in the verse: 'But managers for once cried, "Hold, enough!" ' (735); 'hang a calf-skin on those recreant lines' (740); 'our men in buckram', and 'penetrable stuff' (1049–50). Byron's main literary standards of reference were fixed thus early. He stood for sound sense as opposed to 'strain'd invention' (851) and the general itch to newness and personal excitement impelling contemporary letters. Fear of being 'trite' had ruined poetry:

> *Yet Truth sometimes will lend her noblest fires,*
> *And decorate the verse herself inspires . . .*
>
> (855)

The desire is for a more solid, more practical, more ethical, poetry.

Objections rise to our minds. Among his contemporaries, Byron attacks Wordsworth, Coleridge and Southey, and approves of Crabbe (857), Scott's 'hallow'd harp' (934), 'melodious Rogers' (803), Campbell (801), and Gifford (819–30). Surely he has chosen wrong? Can the work of Scott, Rogers, Campbell and Gifford be said to have survived? Is even Crabbe a deeply important writer to us? Conversely, are not Wordsworth and Coleridge at least as well known as Byron himself? Yes. But we must observe that Byron is not satisfied with his favourites, and is concerned to rouse them to do better justice to their abilities (Scott, 931–2; Campbell, 801; Rogers, 803; Gifford, 819, 829; Sheridan, 582–3; Moore, 294). Moreover, since it is clear that Byron's own work has been under-rated, it may be that some of these lesser figures have suffered an injustice in their degree. For the rest, we may best read this first statement less as a judgement on individuals than as the definition of a critical standpoint. Certain objections regarding Byron's dislike of the 'Lakers' we shall discuss later: he certainly recognized the genius of Coleridge and Wordsworth (pp. 122, 127 below).

What is important is Byron's extraordinary desire, at this youthful age, for a more traditional poetry. He was deeply anxious. He deplores 'the degradation of our vaunted stage', and asks, 'is all sense of shame and talent gone?' (575–6). He writes, moreover, in a strangely avuncular fashion, encouraging and urging on established writers many years his senior, as though they were school-boys; praising, but asking them to mend their ways. What must Scott and the others have thought of this youthful moralist? For moralist he is, not alone in his will to reawaken a past nobility in letters, but in a more strict sense also. Though admiring Moore as the 'young Catullus of his day', he deplores his licentiousness, calling his verses 'melodious advocates of lust' (287–90). And if his own failings be adduced:

Altho' some kind, censorious friend will say,
'What, art thou better, meddling fool, than they?'
And every brother rake will smile to see
That miracle, a moralist in me.
No matter—when some bard in virtue strong,
Gifford perchance, shall raise the chastening song,
Then sleep my pen for ever!

(697)

The lines condense Byron's continual and reiterated views on his own attacks. Again and again he admitted his own failings, both in morals and in being untrue to the Augustan tradition—the two, converging under the name of Pope, were to him almost the same—whilst remaining uncompromising in the general, the impersonal, statement. Nor did he rate his own statement high, but was genuinely ready, indeed anxious, to give place to one more worthy than himself to chastise the age. He was, from the start, half-willing, or more, to stop writing, and asserts that he intended to publish no record of the travels on which he was shortly to embark:

But should I back return, no tempting press
Shall drag my journal from the desk's recess.

(1023)[1]

He often later talked of retiring from authorship. We could say that he wrote, and published, in his own despite.

We may observe Byron's natural assumption of what might be called a civic, or patriotic, responsibility, indicating a certain humility such as you find in Pope, but scarcely in Blake, Wordsworth, or Shelley. Pope and Byron claim less, in a way, for themselves; they speak as mouthpieces of a living, yet traditional, order, not as lonely, self-inspired or God-inspired, prophets. You see it in such a phrase as Pope's 'My Country's Ruin makes me grave'.[2] You have it in Byron's:

For me, who, thus unask'd, have dared to tell
My country what her sons should know too well,
Zeal for her honour bade me here engage
The host of idiots that infest her age;
No just applause her honour'd name shall lose,
As first in freedom, dearest to the Muse.
Oh! would thy bards but emulate thy fame,
And rise more worthy, Albion, of thy name!
What Athens was in science, Rome in power,
What Tyre appeared in her meridian hour,
'Tis thine at once, fair Albion! to have been—
Earth's chief Dictatress, Ocean's lovely Queen:
But Rome decay'd, and Athens strewed the plain,
And Tyre's proud piers lie shattered in the main;
Like these, thy strength may sink, in ruin hurled,
And Britain fall, the bulwark of the world.

(991)

He is thinking, and feeling, nationally, as a patriot, before assuming his satiric mantle. Byron is to be sternly dissociated from the more

[1] This couplet is an improved version of the original, composed after Byron's return. See Hartley Coleridge's note.
[2] *Sat., Epilogue*, II, 207.

obviously 'national' poets, Shakespeare, Milton, Tennyson; he was, or soon became, international, and therein lies much of his importance; but it is worth noting that, whatever his later attacks on Britain, his was an internationalism based on a preliminary patriotism.

No sensitive reader of this poem, and certainly no one attuned to the rest of Byron's work, will waste time on any suspicion of the poet's emotional integrity. Though it is sometimes said that these catapults of criticism were motivated by the review of his own *Hours of Idleness*, yet an early version, entitled *British Bards*, had been composed, and publication intended, before ever the review appeared (*Works*, *Poetry*, ed. Hartley Coleridge, I, 293); and in any case *Hours of Idleness* was itself pregnant with the values we are discussing, and what was done in its cause was done also for the tradition; and so we need not be surprised to recognize in the later poem, throughout all its more important passages, the impersonal anger of great satire. These themselves constitute an honourable part of the tradition which they defend. So pregnant of wit and wisdom, and technically so excellent in point and balance, in choice of word and compactness of line, in swinging, speeding couplets, in paragraph control, they inevitably recall Pope in both manner and statement, though Byron's manner is never quite Pope's, and his vaster genius, together with the complexities and tumult of his time, drew him to wider fields.

With *English Bards and Scotch Reviewers* we naturally group *Hints from Horace*, a work more purely academic in conception akin to Pope's *Essay on Criticism*. This poem was composed in Greece in 1811, but not published till 1831. In it astute comments are made on the literary situation in general and drama in particular, Shakespeare and Milton being used as prototypes as Pope uses Homer and Virgil. Byron himself regarded *Hints from Horace* as more important than *Childe Harold*, and his respect for it was maintained.[1] We need not subscribe to his judgement; but, though its artistic merit falls below his first satire, its interest for the student of Byron's literary theory remains considerable, and, were that, rather than Pope, our present concern, we should give it an extended hearing.

More relevant to our immediate purpose are Byron's literary relations with Leigh Hunt. He admired Hunt's work in conception, but was dubious of his style: of one of his odes he told Murray that its thoughts were good 'but the expressions *buckram*'.[2] He was

[1] Murray, 11 Jan., 1821: LJ, v, 221. [2] April, 1814: LJ, III, 69.

excited about *Rimini*, and wrote to Hunt on 22 October, 1815,[1] urging him to complete it whilst the inspiration was active, but offered certain criticisms, which he called merely 'verbal', with regard to an 'occasional quaintness and obscurity, and a kind of a harsh and yet colloquial compounding of epithets, as if to avoid saying common things in a common way.' Hunt's reply (30 Oct., 1815) is interesting. He defended himself

'in vindication of a theory which I have got on the subject, and by which it appears to me that the original part of my style—if the attempt to bring back an idiomatic spirit in verse can be so called—must stand or fall.'

(LJ, III, 418)

He did, however, admit a horror of the 'prosaic' and the 'eccentric', and invited further discussion, and in his turn offered some criticisms of Byron, who, he says, had 'the complete thing in point of feeling and character—why not, always, in point of words?' He continues:

'The plain matter is this: it appears to me that we often hurt the effect, in modern poetry, of very true feelings and descriptions by putting them in false language, that is to say, we accommodate ourselves to certain habitual, sophisticated phrases of *written* language, and thus take away from real feeling of any sort, the only language it *ever actually uses*, which is the *spoken* language.'

(LJ, III, 418)

The two were clearly at cross-purposes: each admired the other's substance, whilst rejecting his style, or diction. Each thought the other's style *artificial*. Byron's reply (about Nov., 1815) ran:

'I have not had time to attack your *system*, which ought to be done, were it only because it is a *system*. So, by and by, have at you.'

(LJ, III, 248)

To Byron, Hunt's style was a vulgarity. He recalled later how, though admiring *Rimini*, he had from the start remonstrated against its 'vulgarisms', and when Hunt referred to his 'system', then, says Byron, he 'said no more'.[2]

The argument is confusing. Byron himself, in both his dramas and *Don Juan*, was to use an informal, at times a colloquial, manner. Of

[1] LJ, III, 226.
[2] The Bowles Controversy, LJ, v, 588.

his dramatic style, he wrote to Murray on 14 July, 1821: 'It has been my object to be as simple and severe as Alfieri, and I have broken down the *poetry* as nearly as I could to common language'.[1] But notice that the aim is simplicity and that the 'poetry' exists first, to be 'broken down'; the result is to be attained not by working up a colloquial idiom into poetry, but by whittling down an established diction to make a style both literary and colloquial which draws no attention to itself as either. That, anyway, was what Byron wanted: it was to be transparent, like a 'clear spring, bubbling in the sun'.[2] He was in this following Pope, whose poetic story shows a similar development, and the difference from what Hunt was doing will be clear.

It is also clear that Byron, too, could appear to subscribe to a system. But, though so much of a classicist, both in his life-long support of Pope and in his later theories of composition, that his natural tendency was to repudiate any systemization may be seen from his comment on Bowles' *Invariable Principles of Poetry* (1819):

'I do hate that word "*invariable*". What is there of *human*, be it poetry, philosophy, wit, wisdom, science, power, glory, mind, matter, life, or death, which is "*invariable*"? Of course, I put things divine out of the question.'

(The Bowles Controversy, LJ, v, 543)

Whatever Byron, or his diction, or literary theories, stood for, it was not really definable as a system: it was not thought out, not invented. However 'literary' it may appear to us, to him it was already an authentic part and parcel of life, and in supporting what he felt to be a dying tradition, he was trying to preserve what was to him, quite simply, an accepted sovereignty. Above all, he was trying to preserve the *dignity* of poetry. In contrast, Hunt, in both theory and practice, appeared to represent a deliberate vulgarization and a debasing of coinage; and it is the more necessary to labour the point, since we naturally, after a long period of romantic influence and democratic acceptance, tend to believe that such theories as those of Wordsworth and Hunt, since in this they were at one, are the

[1] LJ, v, 323.

[2] Murray, 4 July, 1821; LJ, v, 218. See my article in *The Times Literary Supplement*, 3 Feb., 1950. Extended studies of Byron's dramatic work by Patricia Ball and B. Taborski await publication.

final and only wisdom. It is important to realize that they are not.[1]

Byron's considered views on Hunt are given in a remarkable and fascinating letter to Moore on 1 June, 1818:

'*Hunt's* letter is probably the exact piece of vulgar coxcombry you might expect from his situation. He is a good man, with some poetical elements in his chaos; but spoilt by the Christ-Church Hospital and a Sunday Newspaper—to say nothing of the Surrey gaol, which conceited him into a martyr. But he is a good man. When I saw *Rimini* in MS, I told him that I deemed it good poetry at bottom, disfigured only by a strange style. His answer was, that his style was a system, or *upon system*, or some such cant; and when a man talks of system, his case is hopeless: so I said no more to him, and very little to anyone else.

'He believes his trash of vulgar phrases tortured into compound barbarisms to be *old* English; and we may say of it as Aimwell says of Captain Gibbet's regiment, when the Captain calls it an "old corps" —"the oldest in Europe if I may judge by your uniform". He sent out his *Foliage* by Percy Shelley . . . and, of all the ineffable Centaurs that were ever begotten by Self-love upon a Night-mare, I think "this monstrous Sagittary" the most prodigious. *He* (Leigh Hunt) is an honest charlatan, who has persuaded himself into a belief of his own impostures, and talks Punch in pure simplicity of heart, taking himself (as poor Fitzgerald said of *him*self in the *Morning Post*) for *Vates* in both senses, or nonsenses, of the word. Did you look at the translations of his own which he prefers to Pope or Cowper, and says so?—Did you read his skimble-skamble about Wordsworth being at the head of his own *profession*, in the *eyes* of *those* who followed it? I thought that poetry was an *art*, or an *attribute*, and not a *profession*;—but be it one, is that . . . at the head of *your* profession in *your* eyes? I'll be curst if he is of *mine*, or ever shall be. He is the only one of us (but of us he is not) whose coronation I would oppose. Let them take Scott, Campbell, Crabbe, or you, or me, or any of the living, and throne him;—but not this new Jacob Behmen, this . . . whose pride might have kept him true, even had his principles turned as perverted as his *soi-disant* poetry.

[1] In this connection it may be worth noting that Middleton Murry observes 'how different is Keats' conception of naturalness in poetry from that of a Wordsworth or a Leigh Hunt, intent on "the real language of real people"' (*Keats and Shakespeare*, v, 59).

'But Leigh Hunt is a good man, and a good father—see his Odes to all the Masters Hunt;—a good husband—see his Sonnet to Mrs. Hunt; a good friend—see his Epistles to different people;—and a great coxcomb and a very vulgar person in every thing about him. But that is not his fault, but of circumstances.'

(LJ, IV, 237)

Elsewhere Byron limits the charge of vulgarity to Hunt's literary style, saying that he is 'anything but a vulgar man', and again: 'Of my friend Hunt, I have already said, that he is anything but vulgar in his manners.'[1] As for our letter, to which we shall return, observe particularly the references to 'self-love' and 'nightmare'; and also the humorous capital made from Hunt's more personal poems. The attack is levelled against a certain kind of presumptuous individualism, and is not without relevance to the artistic confusions of our own century.

Hunt's poetry cannot be said to have survived, but Byron's complaint is basically the same with, variously, Wordsworth and Keats, though he acquits Wordsworth and Southey of 'vulgarity'.[2] We must not forget that Byron knew nothing of *The Prelude*, as yet unpublished, and had only Wordsworth's shorter poems and *The Excursion* on which to base his judgements. Nor are all his comments derogatory. On 7 September, 1814, he told Murray:

'There must be many "fine things" in Wordsworth, but I should think it difficult to make *six* quartos (the amount of the whole) all fine, particularly the Pedlar's portion of the poem; but there can be no doubt of his powers to do almost any thing.'

(LJ, III, 131)

To Leigh Hunt on 30 October, 1815, he wrote:

'I take leave to differ with you on Wordsworth, as freely as I once agreed with you; at that time I gave him credit for a promise which is unfulfilled. I still think his capacity warrants all you say of *it* only, but that his performances since *Lyrical Ballads* are miserably inadequate to the ability which lurks within him: there is undoubtedly much natural talent spilt over the *Excursion*; but it is rain upon rocks—where it stands and stagnates; or rain upon sands—where it falls without fertilizing.'

(LJ, III, 238)

[1] The Bowles Controversy, LJ, V, 588, 591.

[2] Ibid., 591.

It is a matter of 'natural talent'; that is, individual, personal, ability; but without any contacts with what Byron felt to be the organic body of traditional poetry; and hence infertile, 'rain upon rocks'. He does not, however, deny the 'rain', the personal ability. His attention was mainly on

> *A drowsy-frowsy poem, call'd the 'Excursion',*
> *Writ in a manner which is my aversion.*
>
> (*Don Juan*, III, 94)

In this matter we must be honest with ourselves. We have all read Wordsworth's *Excursion* through once, and can point to our favourite passages, but how often have we returned to it, as a whole?

With Keats, the problem was different. Byron's antipathy was roused in part by what he considered the tawdry excesses of Hunt's 'Cockney' school: 'it is in their *finery*', he says, that they 'are *most* vulgar'.[1] The excess of decoration in *Endymion* is a good example of the kind of poetry Pope decried in his *Essay on Criticism* as 'false eloquence', spreading its 'gaudy colours' too thick (311–12), though it is of course true that such a fecundity in a young writer may be a sign of genius. There was much in *Endymion* to repel Byron. The heavily enjambed couplets may have appeared almost as an *attack* on a medium about which he felt, as we shall see (p. 134), strongly; and indeed, this may be, in its way, some sort of justification for what is otherwise an unaccountable phenomenon, since the poetry is always labouring to produce rhymes which the enjambments simultaneously kill. One feels a semi-conscious revulsion from the couplet at work, though this same tendency becomes elsewhere a carefree and buoyant freedom, which is inoffensive enough.

But there was a yet more cogent reason for Byron's annoyance, He deeply resented Keats' strictures on the Augustans in *Sleep and Poetry*, which he saw as a piece of unwarrantable *hubris* from 'a young person learning to write poetry and beginning by teaching the art'.[2] Keats was one of those who 'decry Pope', having 'written some lines against him, of which it were better to be the subject than the author'; one who, as a young man, had 'set out with assailing the Poet whom of all others a young aspirant ought to respect and honour and study'; who regarded the succession of great names from

[1] Ibid., 591.

[2] *Blackwood's* Defence, LJ, IV, 491.

Dryden to Johnson as 'a School of dolts'; [1] and who was accordingly labouring under a 'distortion of intellect'.[2] Keats was, of course, fighting for his own poetry, and we may compare T. S. Eliot's statement that when a poet writes as a critic, we must be prepared to find him 'trying to defend the kind of poetry he is writing, or to formulate the kind that he wants to write'.[3] But we must not allow our appreciation of Keats to cloud our understanding, nor regard Byron's private letters, though neither the *Blackwood's* Defence nor the Bowles Controversy come under this heading, on this, or any other subject, as a public unkindness. He always spoke out with force and vigour. He noted in the letter to Hunt which we have already (p. 122) quoted for its remarks on Wordsworth that: 'I write in great haste and, I doubt, *not* much to the purpose; but you have it hot and hot, just as it comes, and so let it go.' [4] That is true, too, of certain more heated utterances on Keats in the letters. We must recognize that his anger was directly proportional to his love of Pope and irritation at the contemporary denigrations.

He was, however, saddened by the news of Keats' death. On 26 April, 1821, he wrote to Shelley with reference to the second of his two public letters to Bowles [5] which he had recently sent off for publication: 'Had I known that Keats was dead—or that he was alive and so sensitive—I should have omitted some remarks upon his poetry, to which I was provoked by his *attack* upon *Pope*, and my disapprobation of *his own* style of writing.' [6] He next arranged to cut out—and the action was characteristic of his behaviour in such matters [7]—his more incisive criticisms, among them some of those which we have just used, together with a number of quotations from Keats' work that told strongly in favour of his own argument. Here is the opening of one of them:

> *The hearty grasp that sends a pleasant sonnet*
> *Into the brain ere one can think upon it;*
> *The silence when some rhymes are coming out;*
> *And when they're come the* very pleasant rout . . .
>
> (LJ, v, 588, note)

[1] The phrase occurs in Keats' *Sleep and Poetry*, 196–7. Pope is not specifically mentioned. The attack is on 'the school'.

[2] The Bowles Controversy, LJ, v, 588; 589, note.

[3] *The Music of Poetry*, W. P. Ker Memorial Lecture, Glasgow, 1942.

[4] LJ, III, 241.

[5] Dated 25 March, 1821; LJ, v, 567.

[6] LJ, v, 268.

[7] See *Lord Byron: Christian Virtues*, III, 122–3.

The lines occur at *Sleep and Poetry* (319). The underlinings appear to be Byron's. His arguments cannot be followed without an honest facing of such lines. Even so, he had very freely admitted Keats' powers of 'imagination', which he saw as having been misdirected by false guides who should feel remorse at having perverted a young man of promise.[1] It must be remembered that Byron is not writing of Keats' 1820 volume, which contained *Hyperion* and the great odes. Of *Hyperion*, he wrote later, after Keats' death, in a manuscript note to his *Blackwood's* Defence dated 12 November, 1821:

'My indignation at Mr. Keats' depreciation of Pope has hardly permitted me to do justice to his own genius, which, malgré all the fantastic fopperies of his style, was undoubtedly of great promise. His fragment of *Hyperion* seems actually inspired by the Titans, and is as sublime as Aeschylus. He is a loss to our literature; and the more so, as he himself, before his death, is said to have been persuaded that he had not taken the right line, and was reforming his style upon the more classical models of the language.'

(LJ, IV, 491, note)

The thought recurs in *Don Juan* (XI, 60), where Keats is said to have died 'just as he really promised something great'. Byron's position is clear. He would naturally have liked the austere diction and comparative reserve of *Hyperion*, and would have approved the poet's submission of himself to the telling of an objective story whose contours are unblurred by any overplus of decoration; while the change to blank verse left the couplet in peace. Had both lived, and most assuredly had they met, there might have been little to quarrel over.

We can say nothing like that of his relations with Wordsworth and Southey. To them Byron's opposition was not merely literary. In literature Wordsworth and Coleridge had broken with tradition; but it was not just the break, but rather *the will to break*, the will to revolution, that so clearly distinguishes them from Byron. They were men of extremes: Wordsworth's *Borderers* and Coleridge's *Remorse* studiously elaborate through their darker, but not wholly unsympathetic, persons a daring Satanism beside which the Byronic heroes and Nietzsche's Zarathustra appear like Victorian moralists; and there may have been good reason to leave *The Borderers* unpublished. Wordsworth's passionate delight in the French Revolution

[1] The Bowles Controversy, LJ, V, 589, note.

and the Coleridge-Southey scheme of Pantisocracy witnessed a youthful will to revolution and a throwing over of traditional forms, customs and values which may be related to the philosophy of Godwin and the poetic idealism of Shelley, but corresponded to nothing in Byron. Byron held strong revolutionary convictions, but only in so far as revolution fulfilled the traditions of civilization as he saw them and served to guard its basic values. He had, like Pope, or Burke, both sides of the opposition steadily in mind; and this was so at all periods of his life; and, since there was nothing superficial about his revolutionary ardour, it persisted undimmed. He himself could never have become a political reactionary. So, when he saw Wordsworth and Southey reacting from their early heterodoxies to a conformation as extreme as their youthful fantasies, he regarded them as little better than a pair of unprincipled time-servers:

'Wordsworth's place may be in the Customs—it is, I think, in that or the Excise—besides another at Lord Lonsdale's table, where this poetical charlatan and political parasite licks up the crumbs with a hardened alacrity; the converted Jacobin having long subsided into the clownish sycophant of the worst prejudices of the aristocracy.'

(Note to *Don Juan*, I, Dedication, 6)

Whether or not Byron did Wordsworth and Southey an injustice does not here concern us. He could admit their poetic powers:

You're shabby fellows—true—but poets still,
And duly seated on the immortal hill.

(*Don Juan*, I, Dedication, 6)

But the rest he could not forgive. He himself had never known, at least in politics, what it was to be either young or irresponsible, as his early notes to the second canto of *Childe Harold* witness, and he could not himself understand the waverings of lesser minds—lesser, I mean, on such issues as these—than his own. It is important that we recognize all that was involved in his general distaste for 'the Lakers', and meanwhile we must never forget that he had neither *The Prelude* nor Wordsworth's later, more impersonal, poetry, the poetry of the *Ecclesiastical Sonnets*,[1] under survey. He himself thought naturally in terms of a unity involving both poetry and politics,

[1] That I do not underrate Wordsworth's later poetry should be clear from my account of his life's work in *The Starlit Dome*.

though the poetry and the politics are beyond party.[1] To Pope and Byron poetry and state-affairs were indissolubly related, while the poetry, in subject, diction, and technique, contains and subsumes, from start to finish, all those party tensions it is to resolve.

Such poetry will be at once traditional and liberal, aristocratic and simple. The poetry of Pope and Byron, at least where style is concerned and complexities involved, is certainly simpler and more readily to be understood by the less educated than are the major works of a Blake, Wordsworth, or Coleridge; and as for subject, there is, in Byron anyway, nearly always enough of objective reference to myth or history to make communication the easier. Though throughout deeply engaged in the eternal dimension, his higher flights, with the possible exception of *Manfred*, are close pinned to earth; and even *Manfred* relies on a well-known pattern of remorse, devils, and damnation, though the hero is not damned. We can see why Byron wrote off Wordsworth as 'this arch-apostle of mystery and mysticism',[2] and made fun of Coleridge

Explaining metaphysics to the nation—
I wish he would explain his explanation.
(*Don Juan*, I, Dedication, 2)

Byron's own handling of the ultimate mysteries, as I have shown in *Byron's Dramatic Prose* (see p. 150, note, below), tended to avoid metaphysical speculation. But it would be an error to suppose that he was lacking in metaphysical insight. Despite his avowed opposition to romanticism, he understood Coleridge's poetry better than any one of his period, once coupling him with Crabbe as one of the two first of contemporary poets, praising the *Ancient Mariner* with fervour, encouraging him to complete *Christabel*, and being alone responsible for the survival of *Kubla Khan*, in which the author himself saw no significance, and probably of *Christabel* too.[3] These presumably won his acceptance by their firmly realized and firmly objective use of symbolism and atmosphere. What Byron disliked in poetry was anything too vague or personal, too far removed from the concrete solidities of poetic creation, regarding all such individualistic and abstract excursions as the direct way to a romantic agony,

[1] For Byron's political thinking, see D. N. Raymond's *Political Career of Lord Byron* (1924); V. de S. Pinto's *Byron and Liberty* (Nottingham, 1944); and *Lord Byron: Christian Virtues*, III.

[2] Hunt, 30 Oct., 1815: LJ, III, 239.

[3] *Lord Byron: Christian Virtues*, II, 59–60.

as when his criticism of Hunt's poetry is couched in terms of 'self-love' and 'nightmare' (p. 121), or when he observes in Keats 'a sort of mental masturbation', together with a 'soliciting his own ideas into a state which is neither poetry nor any thing else', leading direct to 'Bedlam'.[1] All this follows closely the criticism which Swift in *The Battle of the Books* levelled at the moderns, when he contrasted their self-exuded poisons with the objective, bee-like activities of the ancients, making from this or that flower 'honey and wax' as a means to 'sweetness and light'.

We, in our day, are even more deeply self-centred; we, too, hanker after a colloquial idiom, like Wordsworth and Hunt; we, too, have seen in every field of art works which appear to be 'begotten by self-love upon a nightmare' (p. 121). And yet we have also watched T. S. Eliot rather tentatively asserting the aristocratic values and directly insisting on tradition; though the tradition he means is not Pope's or Byron's. His 'classic' principles, however, are not far from those on which Byron constructed his plays. Byron's later diction, as surely as Pope's, aimed at lucidity and simplicity, and both he and Eliot steer clear of those fantastic originalities to which a too personal theory or 'system' may lead the devotee, even though the system may derive from a search for the colloquial.

Byron was not, of course, out to attempt any such transcendental flights as those of a Blake or a Wordsworth. But here again we only see how closely he is with Pope in his steady will to inject poetry into the human situation, psychological and political, before reaching out beyond man's natural sphere; though, as in Pope too, the transcendencies are never denied, continually suggested, and at choice moments colour the human drama with a moving splendour.

II

We shall next discuss more exactly Byron's reverence for Pope. He regularly regarded his own work as miserably inadequate in comparison, without apparently recognizing how far its manner and diction preserved, in all its variations, the values he believed were being lost. Nor did he recognize how much more tumultuous a world he was himself labouring to master, but, with a characteristic integrity, refused excuses, while keeping his eye steadily on the ideal.

[1] Murray, 9 Nov., 1820: SP, ed. Peter Quennell, II, 536; LJ, V, 117, omitting 'masturbation'.

That was to be found in Pope, whom he regarded as the universal poet of mankind.

Writing to Murray on 15 September, 1817, we find him regarding *Childe Harold* as the best he would ever do, and suggesting, as so often, retirement from composition. Then, after an astute comment on Moore's *Lalla Rookh*, he continues:

'With regard to poetry in general, I am convinced, the more I think of it, that he and *all* of us—Scott, Southey, Wordsworth, Moore, Campbell, I,—are all in the wrong, one as much as another; that we are upon a wrong revolutionary poetical system, or systems, not worth a damn in itself, and from which none but Rogers and Crabbe are free; and that the present and next generations will finally be of this opinion. I am the more confirmed in this by having lately gone over some of our classics, particularly *Pope*, whom I tried in this way —I took Moore's poems and my own and some others, and went over them side by side with Pope's, and I was really astonished (I ought not to have been so) and mortified at the ineffable distance in point of sense, harmony, effect and even *Imagination*, passion, and *Invention*, between the little Queen Anne's man, and us of the Lower Empire. Depend upon it, it is all Horace then, and Claudian now, among us; and if I had to begin again, I would model myself accordingly.'

(LJ, IV, 169)

On 2 February, 1818, he addressed Moore on the subject:

'I don't know what Murray may have been saying or quoting. I called Crabbe and Sam the fathers of present Poesy, and said, that I thought—except them—*all* of "*us youth*" were on a wrong tack. But I never said that we did not sail well. Our fame will be hurt by *admiration* and *imitation*. When I say *our*, I mean *all* (Lakers included), except the postscript of the Augustans. The next generation (from the quantity and facility of imitation) will tumble and break their necks off our Pegasus, who runs away with us; but we keep the *saddle*, because we broke the rascal and can ride. But though easy to mount, he is the devil to guide; and the next fellows must go back to the riding-school and the manège, and learn to ride the "great horse".

'Talking of horses . . .'

(LJ, IV, 196)

It is admitted that Crabbe and Rogers are merely a 'postscript'; and he is perfectly well aware of the greatness of romantic poetry. His point was, simply, that the 'romantic' manner had little permanent value, whereas the other had. His anger at the misvaluing of Pope grew fiercer. He would defend him 'against the world'. He attacks 'the new School of Critics and Scribblers, who think themselves poets because they do *not* write like Pope'. He feels personally about it, continually returning to the subject in his letters to Murray:

'I have no patience with such cursed humbug and bad taste; your whole generation are not worth a canto of *The Rape of the Lock*, or the *Essay on Man*, or the *Dunciad*, or "anything that is his".'

(12 April, 1818; LJ, IV, 225)

Again:

'*Read him*—most of you *don't*—but *do*—and I will forgive you: though the inevitable consequence would be that you would burn all I have ever written, and all your other wretched Claudians of the day (except Scott and Crabbe) into the bargain.'

(25 Jan., 1819; LJ, IV, 278)

Again, with reference to Francis Hodgson:

'He is right in defending *Pope* against the bastard Pelicans of the poetical winter day, who add insult to their parricide by sucking the blood of the parent of English *real* poetry—poetry without fault—and then spurning the bosoms which fed them.'

(18 May, 1819; LJ, IV, 304)

And, last:

'Herewith you will receive a note (enclosed) on Pope, which you will find tally with a part of the text of last Post. I have at last lost all patience with the atrocious cant and nonsense about Pope, with which our present blackguards are overflowing, and am determined to make such head against it as an Individual can, by prose or verse; and I will at least do it with good will. There is no bearing it any longer; and if it goes on, it will destroy what little good writing or taste remains amongst us. I hope there are still a few men of taste to second me; but if not, I'll battle it alone, convinced that it is in the best cause of English literature.'

(29 March, 1820; LJ, IV, 425)

In thus championing the tradition Byron was paradoxically acting as an individualist.

But his solitary battle gave him no pleasure. He was deeply pained, and far more truly concerned than about his own work or his friends'. His peculiarly objective concern for literary matters is obvious always, but this goes deeper. Pope stood for something which he regarded as all-important: it was no mere question of 'style'. As one of our quotations (p. 129) shows, Pope's poetry meant to him 'sense', 'harmony', 'effect', 'imagination', 'passion', 'invention': he was thinking of the whole rich, pulsing, solid achievement in all its human wisdom and excelling powers; of Pope's created world. Moreover, as we shall see, politics were involved too, and also ethic. Pope had occupied that specifically liberal yet classical-traditional territory, at once heroic and pacific, which Byron himself inherited.

Before passing to his more elaborated praise of Pope in the Bowles Controversy, we must notice Byron's lengthy statement on the literary situation, from his answer, dated 15 March, 1820,[1] to an attack in *Blackwood's Magazine*, which I call, here and elsewhere, his '*Blackwood's* Defence'. This is the 'note' referred to in Byron's letter to Murray of 29 March, 1820, from which we have just quoted.

He starts by charging his age with the corruption of poetry and continues:

> 'The great cause of the present deplorable state of English poetry is to be attributed to that absurd and systematic depreciation of Pope, in which, for the last few years, there has been a kind of epidemical concurrence. Men of the most opposite opinions have united upon this topic. Warton and Churchill began it, having borrowed the hint probably from the heroes of the *Dunciad*, and their own internal conviction that their proper reputation can be as nothing till the most perfect and harmonious of poets—he who, having no fault, has had REASON made his reproach—was reduced to what they conceived to be his level; but even *they* dared not degrade him below Dryden.'
>
> (LJ, IV, 485)

Byron himself, naturally, intends no slight against Dryden.

We pass to some aspersions on the works of Southey and Wordsworth with a thrust at Wordsworth's prefaces 'couched in such prose

[1] LJ, IV, 474.

as must give peculiar delight to those who have read the prefaces of Pope and Dryden, scarcely less celebrated for the beauty of their prose than for the charms of their verse'. Coleridge is, as elsewhere, let off more lightly and his poetry respected. But all three are guilty on the main charge, involving Pope:

'These three personages, Southey, Wordsworth, and Coleridge, had all of them a very natural antipathy to Pope; and I respect them for it, as the only original feeling or principle which they have contrived to preserve. But they have been joined in it by those who have joined them in nothing else: by the Edinburgh Reviewers, by the whole heterogeneous mass of living English poets, excepting Crabbe, Rogers, Gifford and Campbell, who, both by precept and practice, have proved their adherence; and by me, who have shamefully deviated in practice, but have ever loved and honoured Pope's poetry with my whole soul, and hope to do so till my dying day. I would rather see all I have ever written lining the same trunk in which I actually read the eleventh book of a modern epic poem at Malta, in 1811 (I opened it to take out a change after the paroxysm of a tertian, in the absence of my servant, and found it lined with the name of the maker, Eyre, Cockspur Street, and with the epic poetry alluded to) than sacrifice what I firmly believe in as the Christianity of English poetry, the poetry of Pope.'

(LJ, IV, 486)

There cannot be many examples of a major poet so slighting his own life's work in order to safeguard the reputation of an earlier master.

Then follow more thrusts at the poetry of Wordsworth and Southey and a sharp denial, with evidence drawn from the past, that contemporary popularity argues a lack of poetic genius. Here is the rest:

'It may be asked, why, having this opinion of the present state of poetry in England and having had it long, as my friends and others well knew—possessing, or having possessed too, as a writer, the ear of the public for the time being—I have not adopted a different plan in my own compositions, and endeavoured to correct rather than encourage the taste of the day. To this I would answer, that it is easier to perceive the wrong than to pursue the right, and that I have never contemplated the prospect "of filling (with *Peter Bell*, see its Preface) permanently a station in the literature of the country".

Those who know me best, know this, and that I have been considerably astonished at the temporary success of my works, having flattered no person and no party, and expressed opinions which are not those of the general reader. Could I have anticipated the degree of attention which has been accorded me, assuredly I would have studied more to deserve it. But I have lived in far countries abroad, or in the agitating world at home, which was not favourable to study or reflection; so that almost all I have written has been mere passion—passion, it is true, of different kinds, but always passion: for in me (if it be not an Irishism to say so) my *indifference* was a kind of passion, the result of experience, and not the philosophy of nature. Writing grows a habit, like a woman's gallantry: there are women who have had no intrigue, but few who have had but one only: so there are millions of men who have never written a book, but few who have written only one. And thus, having written once, I wrote on; encouraged no doubt by the success of the moment, yet by no means anticipating its duration, and I will venture to say, scarcely even wishing it. But then I did other things besides write, which by no means contributed either to improve my writings or my prosperity.

'I have thus expressed publicly upon the poetry of the day the opinion I have long entertained and expressed of it to all who have asked it, and to some who would rather not have heard it: as I told Moore not very long ago, "we are all wrong except Rogers, Crabbe, and Campbell." Without being old in years, I am old in days, and do not feel the adequate spirit within me to attempt a work which should show what I think right in poetry, and must content myself with having denounced what is wrong. There are, I trust, younger spirits rising up in England, who, escaping the contagion which has swept away poetry from our literature, will recall it to their country, such as it once was and may still be.

'In the mean time, the best sign of amendment will be repentance, and new and frequent editions of Pope and Dryden.

'There will be found as comfortable metaphysics, and ten times more poetry in the *Essay on Man*, than in the *Excursion*. If you search for passion, where is it to be found stronger than in the epistle from Eloisa to Abelard, or in *Palamon and Arcite*? Do you wish for invention, imagination, sublimity, character? seek them in the *Rape of the Lock*, the *Fables* of Dryden, the *Ode of Saint Cecilia's Day*, and *Absalom and Achitophel*: you will discover, in these two poets only, *all* for which you must ransack innumerable metres, and God only knows how many *writers* of the day, without finding a tittle of the same qualities—with the addition, too, of wit, of which the latter have none. I have not, however, forgotten *Thomas Brown the Younger* nor the *Fudge Family*, nor Whistlecraft; but that is not wit—it is humour. I will say nothing of the harmony of Pope and Dryden in comparison, for there is not a living poet (except Rogers, Gifford, Campbell, and Crabbe) who can write an heroic couplet. The fact is, that the exquisite beauty of their versification has withdrawn the public attention from their other excellences, as the vulgar eye will rest more upon the splendour of the uniform than the quality of the troops. It is this very harmony, particularly in Pope, which has raised the vulgar and atrocious cant against him:—because his versification is perfect, it is assumed that it is his only perfection; because his truths are so clear, it is asserted that he has no invention; and because he is always intelligible, it is taken for granted that he has no genius. We are sneeringly told that he is the "Poet of Reason", as if this was a reason for his being no poet. Taking passage for passage, I will undertake to cite more lines teeming with *imagination* from Pope than from any *two* living poets, be they who they may. To take an instance at random from a species of composition not very favourable to imagination—Satire: set down the character of Sporus, with all the wonderful play of fancy which is scattered over it, and place by its side an equal number of verses, from any two existing poets, of the same power and the same variety—where will you find them?

'I merely mention one instance of many, in reply to the injustice done to the memory of him who harmonized our poetical language. The attorneys' clerks, and other self-educated genii, found it easier to distort themselves to the new models, than to toil after the symmetry of him who had enchanted their fathers. They were besides smitten by being told that the new school were to revive the language of Queen Elizabeth, the true English: as every body in the reign of Queen Anne wrote no better than French, by a species of literary treason.

'Blank verse, which, unless in the drama, no one except Milton ever wrote who could rhyme, became the order of the day—or else such rhyme as looked still blanker than the verse without it. I am aware that Johnson has said, after some hesitation, that he could not "prevail upon himself to wish that Milton had been a rhymer." The opinions of that truly great man, whom it is also the present fashion to decry, will ever be received by me with that deference which time will restore to him from all; but, with all humility, I am not persuaded that the *Paradise Lost* would not have been more nobly conveyed to posterity, not perhaps in heroic couplets, although even *they* could sustain the subject if well balanced, but in the stanza of Spenser or of Tasso, or in the terza rima of Dante, which the powers of Milton could easily have grafted on our language. The *Seasons* of Thomson would have been better in rhyme, although still inferior to his *Castle of Indolence*; and Mr. Southey's *Joan of Arc* no worse, although it might have taken up six months instead of weeks in the composition. I recommend also to the lovers of lyrics the perusal of the present laureate's *Odes* by the side of Dryden's on Saint Cecilia, but let him be sure to read *first* those of Mr. Southey.

'To the heaven-born genii and inspired young scriveners of the day much of this will appear paradox: it will appear so even to the higher order of our critics; but it was a truism twenty years ago, and it will be a reacknowledged truth in ten more.'

(LJ, IV, 488)

Byron's 'ten' years is an understatement; had he said a couple of hundred he would have been nearer the truth. Such over-optimism appears to be a regular constituent of prophetic talk, from the New Testament on: an eternal truth grasped, its flashing power forces a more rapid interpretation in temporal terms than temporal terms allow.

Our first reaction to this uncompromising statement is likely enough to be hostile. Byron's convictions register with such smashing, yet effortless, force, that we are always in danger of blaming him for his superlative manner. Observe that he at least claims to respect *any* sincerely held opinion, even against Pope. For the rest, there is certainly much sound sense. Coleridge's poetry is respected, but the aspersions on Southey's metrical experiments and fantastic tales are probably just, and the general level of Wordsworth's prose merits much, if not all, of Byron's strictures; compare his famous prefaces with Byron's prose, and the difference in precision and power will be evident. The assessment of the relative merits of the *Essay on Man* and *The Excursion* is not unreasonable, nor is the praise of *Eloisa to Abelard*, to the powers of which Byron was finely sensitive (see pp. 140–1, 151). Moreover, he rates his own work as nothing in comparison with Pope's, admitting himself to be guilty of many of the faults he criticizes. His consideration of Italian as our only *poetical* language (LJ, IV, 487) was so deeply held that he modelled his later style on the Italian and even planned to compose his greatest work in the language,[1] and his own plays were modelled, in both language and structure, on classic principles. Most important of all, he sees and states clearly, with a diagnosis which is one of general critical interest quite apart from our present concern, how and why Pope had been misrepresented, suffering for his technical virtuosity and rational clarity, so that such comparatively minor elements had been allowed, as so often happens in literary criticism, to fog the contours of his major achievement. Finally, observe the respect accorded Johnson, whom he elsewhere calls 'the noblest critical mind which our country has produced',[2] and the high valuation placed upon the couplet.

We shall not, naturally, subscribe to all his judgements in point of detail and emphasis, but we can get the general tenour of his contention and recognize a truth. Pope was 'the Christianity of English poetry' (p. 132); far more than 'taste', as usually understood, was involved; the question was, whether our literature 'shall or shall not relapse into the Barbarism from which it has scarcely emerged for above a century and a half'.[3] The word 'barbarism' is indicative: the Augustan manner is regarded as the voice of civilization.

But we must not remain content with the 'manner'. We have for too long shrivelled the appreciation of Pope, and not Pope only, into talk of style and language in dissociation from the subject-matter; all good enough, and necessary to a specialist enquiry, but not the main thing. Pope himself in his *Essay on Criticism* has carefully warned us of those critics who, 'fond' of some subsidiary interest, 'make the Whole depend upon a Part', some looking merely for 'conceit', and others for 'language', 'sense' being slurred by a concentration on 'style' (263–308):

But most by Numbers judge a Poet's song;
And smooth or rough, with them is right or wrong:
In the bright Muse though thousand charms conspire,
Her voice is all these tuneful fools admire . . .

(337)

They are like those going to church not for the 'doctrine', but for

[1] Murray, 6 April, 1819: LJ, IV, 284. [2] The Bowles Controversy, LJ, V, 564.
[3] Gilchrist, 5 Sept., 1821: SP, II, 666.

the 'music' (343); and the charge would be just as valid were they to be found going to church, as they do today, for discord rather than music. Byron (p. 134) levels a similar indictment against Pope's critics: what he saw in Pope was no mere technical virtuosity but, as one of the letters (p. 129) shows and his *Blackwood's* Defence makes clear, qualities far richer. He was concerned to advertise all the 'thousand charms' of Pope's muse; his close texture of impressions, his play of fancy, his rounded and choice vocabulary, his richly inlaid perceptions; above all, his fine, vigorous, and essentially poetic philosophy, aiming to penetrate and redirect not so much man's thinking as his instincts, whereby he became in Byron's mind the greatest ethical poet of the world.

III

We shall now pass to consider Byron's more expanded arguments on Pope's importance. These occur in the section entitled *Controversy between Byron and Bowles as to the poetry and character of Pope* given in Appendix III (522–92) to the fifth volume of the *Letters and Journals*.[1] Byron composed two extended letters in answer to the Rev. W. L. Bowles' *Invariable Principles of Poetry* (1819). The first was published in 1821;[2] the second, which did not appear in print until 1835, Byron withheld in view of his adversary's good-natured acceptance of his strictures. He asked Murray to thank Bowles for his 'candour and kindness', adding: 'You will of course *not* publish my defence of Gilchrist, as, after Bowles' good humour upon the subject, it would be too savage.'[3] In these letters Byron defends Pope variously against the implications of the *Principles* and the criticisms made upon his life in Bowles' edition of Pope's works (1806), which Byron had already attacked in *English Bards and Scotch Reviewers*:

> *If Pope, whose fame and genius, from the first,*
> *Have foiled the best of critics, needs the worst,*

[1] Tillotson ('Nature', 18, note) refers to the 'early nineteenth-century controversy on Pope's status as poet', which he describes as 'a muddle of vituperation, pedantry, and vital aesthetics'. He notes that 'the history of the controversy has been set out by J. J. van Rennes in *Bowles, Byron and the Pope-Controversy* (1927)'.

[2] Completed 10 Feb., 1821; LJ, v, 201.

[3] Murray, 14 May, 1821; LJ, v, 285–6.

Do thou essay: each fault, each failing scan;
The first of poets was, alas! but man.
Rake from each ancient dunghill every pearl,
Consult Lord Fanny and confide in Curll;
Let all the scandals of a former age
Perch on thy pen, and flutter o'er thy page.

(367)

The disagreement was of some standing, and when Bowles' *Principles* drove home the attack from a new angle, Byron was roused to a reply.

Briefly, Bowles was arguing from a romantic view that nature was in itself a more poetical subject than things made by man. His key statement runs: 'Images drawn from what is beautiful or sublime in nature are *more poetical* than images drawn from art'.[1] The Pyramids and the Great Wall of China, he says, though impressive enough, derive their appeal from natural or moral, and by this he means human and historical, associations: the point is, they are not *in themselves* so poetical.[2] Byron's reply urges the limitations of pure nature. He is not, perhaps, altogether true to his own experiences, which, in prose and poetry alike, record a quivering susceptibility to natural phenomena of certain more titanic kinds; sun, tempests, the ocean, mountains.[3] In engaging in the rather unprofitable argument as to whether a ship is or is not more poetical than the sea, he at least leaves us some good descriptions of actual seas and fleets.[4] But when he urges that the Parthenon is a finer thing than the rock it stands on, and questions the aesthetic value of the desert without its pyramids,[5] he is perhaps not quite fair to Bowles, who was supporting primarily that in nature which was peculiarly 'beautiful' or 'sublime'. Byron develops [6] some interesting appreciations of the arts, architectural and sculptural, of Italy, which, being alive with 'mind', are considered finer than Mont Blanc; and Westminster Abbey and St. Paul's are, as objects, said to hold poetry, apart from all human purposes and associations. The pictorial artist, it is argued, always

[1] LJ, v, 531. [2] LJ, v, 527.

[3] In her *Goethe and Byron* (Byron Foundation Lecture, Nottingham, 1949–50), E. M. Butler makes some interesting comparisons between the mountains, cataracts and sea of *Childe Harold* and the nature-poetry of Goethe's *Faust*. Goethe, she writes, tends 'to contract rather than expand before nature's immensities', whereas 'the diametrically opposite tendency was innate in Byron'.

[4] LJ, v, 543–6. [5] LJ, v, 546–7. [6] LJ, v, 547–52.

improves on nature, if only by choice of view, distance, light: 'Nature, exactly, simply, barely, Nature, will make no great artist of any kind, and least of all a poet.'[1]

The issues are fairly clear and need little discussion. Byron never embraced a poetic pantheism and, though he remains our greatest poet of sun and sea, regarded both rather as symbols of divinity than as themselves divine, as at *Manfred*, III, ii (sun); *Sardanapalus*, II, i (sun; and, later, stars); and *Childe Harold*, IV, 183 (ocean); and in *Manfred* he realizes his part-Alpine and part-spiritual atmosphere through various mythological personifications. He certainly never allowed nature a central, protagonist, importance as rival to divinity or man. It is, however, true that his heavy emphasis here on arts of design does not correspond to their relative importance in his own poetic universe, though they are (see pp. 84, 87) more important than has been properly recognized. He is, of course, thinking not of his own poetry, but of Pope's, and we may, for simplicity, regard as the crux of the matter the game of cards in *The Rape of the Lock*, which Bowles had compared derogatarily with a forest walk as a poetic theme. Byron's answer is important:

> 'To the question, "whether the description of a game of cards be as poetical, supposing the execution of the artists equal, as a description of a walk in a forest?" it may be answered, that the *materials* are certainly not equal; but that "the *artist*", who has rendered the "game of cards poetical", is *by far the greater* of the two. But all this "ordering" of poets is purely arbitrary on the part of Mr. B. There may or may not be, in fact, different "orders" of poetry, but the poet is always ranked according to his execution, and not according to his branch of the art.'
>
> (LJ, V, 552–3)

Again,

> 'Away, then, with this cant about nature, and "invariable principles of poetry!" A great artist will make a block of stone as sublime as a mountain, and a good poet can imbue a pack of cards with more poetry than inhabits the forests of America.'
>
> (LJ, V, 557)

Byron is simply out to defend Pope against those who find in him a dearth of nature poetry.

[1] LJ, V, 550.

That Pope's feeling for nature was powerful enough we have already amply demonstrated, and that it should most often be approached in terms of collaboration with man is surely no just criticism. The desire of Pope's century to make friends with nature is witnessed by their attainments in landscape gardening; and Pope, says Byron, 'was the *first* who ridiculed the "formal French, Dutch, false and unnatural taste in gardening", both in *prose* and verse'. He notes his up-bringing at Windsor and frequent visits to country seats, among them Stowe; that he made 'his own little "five acres" a model to princes'; and that Warton thought that one of the best works of Kent, whom Byron calls 'the first of our artists who imitated nature', was modelled after Pope's example. As for the poetry, Byron asserts that it would be easy by quotation to show that 'no poet ever admired Nature more, or used her better, than Pope has done'; and as for 'schools of poetry', such things are never talked of 'till the decay of the art has increased with the number of its professors'.[1]

Byron is anxious to drive home to his readers the wealth and substance of Pope's imaginative creation. 'His various excellence', he writes, 'is really wonderful: architecture, painting, *gardening*, all are alike subject to his genius';[2] 'architecture' referring to *The Temple of Fame*, from which Byron quotes in his *Blackwood's* Defence. In a letter to Murray written in March, 1821 *apropos* of his answer to Bowles, he wrote: 'I will show more *imagery* in twenty lines of Pope than in any equal length of quotation in English poesy', and, after listing twenty-three images from the lines on Sporus in the *Epistle to Dr. Arbuthnot*, continues:

'Now, is there a line of all the passage without the most *forcible* imagery (for his purpose)? Look at the *variety*, at the *poetry*, of the passage—at the *imagination*: there is hardly a line from which a *painting* might not be made, and *is*. But this is nothing in comparison with his higher passages in the *Essay on Man*, and many of his other poems, serious and comic.

(LJ, v, 259–60)

Or again, he turns—we are back at the Controversy again—to *Eloisa to Abelard*, praising its consummate artistry and delicacy of feeling:

'The "licentiousness" of the story was *not* Pope's—it was a fact. All

[1] LJ, v, 586–7.

[2] LJ, v, 587.

that it had of gross, he has softened;—all that it had of indelicate, he has purified—all that it had of passionate, he has beautified;—all that it had of holy, he has hallowed. Mr. Campbell has admirably marked this in a few words (I quote from memory), in drawing the distinction between Pope and Dryden, and pointing out where Dryden was wanting. "I fear," says he, "that had the subject of Eloisa fallen into his (Dryden's) hands, that he would have given us but a *coarse* draft of her passion." Never was the delicacy of Pope so much shown as in this poem. With the facts and the letters of Eloisa he has done what no other mind but that of the best and purest of poets could have accomplished with such materials. Ovid, Sappho (in the Ode called hers)—all that we have of ancient, all that we have of modern poetry, sinks into nothing compared with him in this production.'

(LJ, v, 581)

It is strange and sad that so little attention should have been accorded this supremely beautiful and powerful work, surely among the first treasures of its kind; if it does not rather stand alone, a kind apart. Bowles himself singled it out for praise (LJ, v, 536).

Our last quotation shows that Byron does not rate Dryden level with Pope; his was not merely an admiration for the neo-classic manner, though that was a constituent; it was, pre-eminently, a fervour inspired by recognition of Pope's status as a man of genius with a message and a meaning of first importance. That is why Bowles' criticism of Pope's character, based mainly on scandal and innuendo, so infuriated him: for, after all, he asked, what do all these 'accumulated hints' amount to? [1] We, in our day of 'debunking', have watched many such attempts, conscious or unconscious, to let biography make small what we deeply know to be great, and it will do us, as literary commentators, no harm to consider Byron's uncompromising condemnation. After answering certain of Bowles' criticisms as to Pope's character, he continues:

'But there is something a little more serious in Mr. Bowles' declaration, that he "*would* have spoken" of his "noble generosity to the outcast Richard Savage", and other instances of a compassionate and generous heart, "*had they occurred to his recollection when he wrote*". What! is it come to this? Does Mr. B. sit down to write a minute and laboured life and edition of a great poet? Does he

[1] LJ, v, 541.

anatomize his character, moral and poetical? Does he present us with his faults and with his foibles? Does he sneer at his feelings, and doubt of his sincerity? Does he unfold his vanity and duplicity? and then omit the good qualities which might, in part, have "covered this multitude of sins"? and then plead that "*they did not occur to his recollection*"? Is this the frame of mind and of memory with which the illustrious dead are to be approached? If Mr. Bowles, who must have had access to all the means of refreshing his memory, did not recollect these facts, he is unfit for his task; but if he *did* recollect and omit them, I know not what he is fit for, but I know what would be fit for him. Is the plea of "not recollecting" such prominent facts to be admitted? Mr. B. has been at a public school, and, as I have been publicly educated also, I can sympathize with his predilection. When we were in the third form even, had we pleaded on the Monday morning that we had not brought up the Saturday's exercise, because "we had forgotten it", what would have been the reply? And is an excuse, which would not be pardoned to a schoolboy, to pass current in a matter which so nearly concerns the fame of the first poet of his age, if not of his country? If Mr. B. so readily forgets the virtues of others, why complain so grievously that others have a better memory for his own faults? They are but the faults of an author; while the virtues he omitted from his catalogue are essential to the justice due to a man.'

(LJ, v, 562)

Again:

'A fulsome editor is pardonable though tiresome, like a panegyrical son whose pious sincerity would demi-deify his father. But a detracting editor is a parricide. He sins against the nature of his office and connection—he murders the life to come of his victim. If his author is not worthy to be remembered, do not edit at all: if he be, edit honestly, and even flatteringly. The reader will forgive the weakness in favour of mortality, and correct your adulation with a smile.'

(LJ, v, 586)

That is a statement of general application, never more needed than today. But Byron solaces himself with the Shakespearian thought that his hero lies beyond such criticism:

'Pope himself "sleeps well"—nothing can touch him further; but those who love the honour of their country, the perfection of her literature, the glory of her language—are not to be expected to permit an atom of his dust to be stirred in his tomb, or a leaf to be stripped from the laurel which grows over it.'

(LJ, v, 568)

Observe the phraseology: 'honour', 'country', 'glory', 'dust', 'laurel'. The diction is poetic, heroic, patriotic; a diction which many of Byron's contemporaries would have been too proud, too self-centred, to use.

Byron speaks a language similar to Pope's, and in both it is the sign of a certain spiritualized aristocracy, a certain fervour, a certain message. It springs from the aristocratic, that is, the civilized, tradition of Renaissance Europe which, in its turn, derives authority from the ancients. There is in it an ethic, however hard to define: to Byron Pope was 'the greatest moral poet of any age, or in any language'; [1] he was not merely a poet wealthy in all the normal resources of the art, but, pre-eminently, a guide to man, as well in his manner as in his matter; virtue was felt to permeate his work. In contrast to Pope's nobility of manner lay what Byron regarded as the vulgarity of the Cockney school:

'The grand distinction of the under forms of the new school of poets is their *vulgarity*. By this I do not mean that they are *coarse*, but "shabby-genteel", as it is termed. A man may be *coarse* and yet not *vulgar*, and the reverse. Burns is often coarse, but never *vulgar*.'

(LJ, v, 591)

The Lake School are, for once, exonerated; it is in their 'finery' that the new school, by which Byron means certain London writers, are 'most vulgar', and

'they may be known by this at once; as what we called at Harrow "a Sunday Blood" might be easily distinguished from a gentleman, although his cloathes might be the better cut, and his boots the best blackened, of the two:—probably because he made the one, or cleaned the other, with his own hands.'

(LJ, v, 591)

There is a sting in that; not, of course, a social sting, but an attack on the writer who has no humility before convention or tradition, as when T. S. Eliot, in our time, compares Blake's philosophy to

[1] LJ, v, 568.

home-made furniture. This London school, followers of Hunt, might well be in themselves 'honourable' and 'gentlemanly', but, if so, such qualities were 'studiously excluded from their publications'. He continues:

'Far be it from me to presume that there ever was, or can be, such a thing as an *aristocracy* of *poets*; but there *is* a nobility of thought and of style, open to all stations, and derived partly from talent, and partly from education—which is to be found in Shakespeare, and Pope, and Burns, no less than in Dante and Alfieri, but which is nowhere to be perceived in the mock birds and bards of Mr. Hunt's little chorus.'

(LJ, v, 591)

He admits that this 'gentlemanliness' is hard to define except by concrete examples, and proceeds to suggest the professions, which may be high or low in social status, which do, and those which do not, appear to have it, with the interesting conclusion that women have more of it than men. It is a poetic necessity:

'In poetry, as well as writing in general, it will never *make* entirely a poet or a poem; but neither poet nor poem will ever be good for anything without it. It is the *salt* of society, and the seasoning of composition. *Vulgarity* is far worse than downright *blackguardism*; for the latter comprehends wit, humour, and strong sense at times; while the former is a sad abortive attempt at all things, "signifying nothing". It does not depend upon low themes, or even low language, for Fielding revels in both;—but is he ever *vulgar*? No. You see the man of education, the gentleman, and the scholar, sporting with his subject—its master, not its slave. Your vulgar writer is always most vulgar the higher his subject, as the man who showed the menagerie at Pidcock's was wont to say—"This, gentlemen, is the *eagle* of the *sun*, from Archangel, in Russia; the *otterer* it is the *igherer* he flies". But to the proof. It is a thing to be felt more than explained. Let any man take up a volume of Mr. Hunt's subordinate writers, read (if possible) a couple of pages, and pronounce for himself, if they contain not the kind of writing which may be likened to "shabby-genteel" in actual life. When he has done this, let him take up Pope; and when he has laid him down, take up the cockneys again—if he can.'

(LJ, v, 591)

The comparison with 'blackguardism' is revealing. We are close to an ethic, but the ethic is not quite a matter of good and evil as normally understood, while even 'blackguardism' may be in part redeemed by 'wit', 'humour' and good 'sense'. With these quotations we may group Byron's well-known letter to Murray of 12 September, 1821:

'The pity of these men is, that they never lived either in *high life*, nor in *solitude*: there is no medium for the knowledge of the *busy* or the *still* world. If admitted into high life for a season, it is merely as *spectators*—they form no part of the Mechanism thereof. Now Moore and I, the one by circumstance, and the other by birth, happened to be free of the corporation, and to have entered into its pulses and passions, *quarum partes fuimus*. Both of us have learnt by this much which nothing else could have taught us.'

(LJ, v, 362)

We are pointed to a balance of humanism and religion. 'Solitude' suggests religion, or its equivalent of meditation and, in general, spirituality; 'high life' suggests the real forces at play among leaders, political or social, who are presumably being distinguished, with a direct reference to 'passions', from a middle-class overlaying the 'pulses' and energies of life with a second-rate and second-hand morality. Whatever our social views, we must be clear as to Byron's meaning. It is something you do not get in sermons or tracts, but you will find it in Castiglione's *Il Cortegiano* and in Nietzsche's *Thus Spake Zarathustra*.

Pope and Byron were torch-bearers of a certain truth, or way of life, a nobility at once personal and civic, humanistic and spiritual, heroic and yet Christian, most hard to characterize, since none of these exists by itself, and each is involved in the rest. We may call them upholders of a tradition, but the term is misleading since this tradition only exists in so far as it is recreated from the centre. Poetic diction may or may not accompany the expression of this 'truth', or way; both Pope and Byron use a less literary speech in their later work. But it remains valuable as a symbol and symptom of the wisdom implied, consisting, as at its best it does, in a choice and use of words which have become through the winnowing of centuries bearers of certain traditional, yet not specifically religious, verities and virtues. Such a diction burns in the noble humility of Byron's acceptance of a possible oblivion when he writes that if destiny bar

My name from out the temple where the dead
Are honour'd by the nations—let it be—
And light the laurels on a loftier head!
And be the Spartan's epitaph on me—
'Sparta hath many a worthier son than he'.
(*Childe Harold*, IV, 10)

It is doubtful whether the exact kind of humility and nobility carried by those lines, whether their exact wave-length, as it were, could be transmitted in a less traditionally heroic, a less aristocratic, diction. The diction is itself constituent to the virtue in question: to use a paradox, the lines are *superbly* humble.

In this period, classical influence bulks large; at other periods other choices might function better. Fine language is a repository of living values, and by acceptance of certain already formed, compact, units of poetry in word or phrase, and beyond that, of certain established areas of thought and emotion, a poet may get to work in a more valuable way than he who despises them, since he is not always melting everything down to remould it nearer to his own heart's desire. He is not starting from scratch and neglecting the twenty or more centuries that have forged his tools. It may, indeed, be sometimes necessary to do that; we seem to be doing it today. But we are also very clearly over-doing it, and Byron's peculiar value and challenge to us lies precisely in his refusal, in his will to preserve, and as it were hurl against the centuries to come, the poetic achievement of Pope.

He does not, however, remain content with vague attempts to characterize a nobility of manner; he claims that Pope is a moral force in a far more precise sense, though we must be on our guard against the dangers inherent in the word 'moral'. His life-long craving was, in every sphere, a craving for moral, including sexual, purity. His youthful lyrics show it; so does his *English Bards and Scotch Reviewers*; his satire *The Waltz* was written from a loathing of public embraces; and the Doge's final denunciation in *Marino Faliero* is barbed with as fierce a puritanical fervour as you will find in English literature. As Hobhouse, long after his death, witnessed, his natural poetic tendency was to deny wrongdoing any attractive quality: 'It will be the eternal praise of his writings, as it was one of the merits of his conversation, that he threw no lustre on any exploit, however brilliant, any character, however exalted, which had not contributed to the happiness or welfare of mankind.'[1] According to Lady Blessington, he felt that, had his genius not been thwarted by opposition, it might have developed into 'one unbroken blaze of light';[2] and by this he would have meant a kind of teaching, or poetic doctrine, a Promethean illumination. In this, he had, in his own eyes, failed; even so, as far as sexual morality was concerned, his poetry was long known as 'the chaste muse of Albion', and the title was correct enough, at least up to the composition of *Beppo*, *Don Juan* and *Sardanapalus*, when he made an advance with full understanding of what he was doing, and why. Of *Don Juan* he wrote:

'If they had told me the poetry was bad, I would have acquiesced; but they say the contrary, and then talk to me about morality—the first time I ever heard the word from anybody who was not a rascal that used it for a purpose. I maintain that it is the most moral of poems; but if people won't discern the moral, that is their fault, not mine.'

(Murray, 1 Feb., 1819; LJ, IV, 279)

We may say that the 'moral' of *Don Juan* exists in terms of (i) its emphasis, in the Juan and Haidée episode, on the innate purity of young love, even without the marriage bond, an emphasis which we may relate to the illicit love of the hero in the deeply considered pattern of *Sardanapalus*; and (ii) the sunny humour shining over a number of episodes where a conventional veneer is stripped from human instincts, showing them, without bitterness, exactly as they are. The critical implications are too complex to discuss here, but we can agree that the 'moral' of *Don Juan* has much to do with its attack on convention, insincerity and 'cant'; and this is what Byron means.

We have accordingly two antithetical but complementary principles active throughout Byron's life and writings. They are: (i) a craving for moral purity, and (ii) a detestation of cant, which was driven to an almost perverted extreme of self-accusation, and in general a refusal to forget, or deny the rights of, all basic passions and compulsions, sexual, social, and political. What he demanded was a righteousness that *left nothing out*; a comprehensive righteousness

[1] *Travels in Albania and other Provinces of Turkey*, J. C. Hobhouse, Lord Broughton; 2nd ed., 1858; vol. I, App. 542; quoted *Lord Byron: Christian Virtues*, II, 95.

[2] *Conversations*, 304.

with, to use Pope's indispensable line, 'wild Nature's vigor working at the root'; [1] at the limit, a sexually-impelled asceticism or purity. He hoped that marriage might give it him, but it could not. In one place only he found what he wanted: in the work of Pope. Pope offered a classic purity in strong contrast to what appeared to him the fungoid growths of those contemporary sects, schools and schisms which he scorned, and this exquisite temple of art contained all that could be desired of passion, ethic and reality. Our cluster of values is well illustrated in a fine passage:

'The attempt of the poetical populace of the present day to obtain an ostracism against Pope is as easily accounted for as the Athenian's shell against Aristides; they are tired of hearing him always called "the Just". They are also fighting for life; for, if he maintains his station, they will reach their own—by falling. They have raised a mosque by the side of a Grecian temple of the purest architecture; and, more barbarous than the barbarians from whose practice I have borrowed the figure, they are not contented with their own grotesque edifice, unless they destroy the prior, and purely beautiful fabric which preceded, and which shames them and theirs for ever and ever. I shall be told that amongst those I *have* been (or it may be still *am*) conspicuous—true, and I am ashamed of it. I *have* been amongst the builders of this Babel, attended by a confusion of tongues, but *never* amongst the envious destroyers of the classic temple of our predecessor. I have loved and honoured the fame and name of that illustrious and unrivalled man, far more than my own paltry renown, and the trashy jingle of the crowd of "Schools" and upstarts, who pretend to rival, or even surpass him. Sooner than a single leaf should be torn from his laurel, it were better that all which these men, and that I, as one of their set, have ever written, should

Line trunks, clothe spice, or, fluttering in a row,
Befringe the rails of Bedlam, or Soho! [2]

There are those who will believe this, and those who will not. You, sir, know how far I am sincere, and whether my opinion, not only in the short work intended for publication,[3] and in private letters which can never be published, has or has not been the same. I look

[1] *Essay on Man*, II, 184. [2] *Horace, Ep.* II, i, 418 (the quotation is inexact).

[3] The work is *Hints from Horace* which had not as yet been published: see Murray, 11 January, 1821; LJ, v, 221.

upon this as the declining age of English poetry; no regard for others, no selfish feeling, can prevent me from seeing this, and expressing the truth. There can be no worse sign for the taste of the times than the depreciation of Pope. It would be better to receive for proof Mr. Cobbett's rough but strong attack upon Shakespeare and Milton, than to allow this smooth and "candid" undermining of the reputation of the most *perfect* of our poets, and the purest of our moralists. Of his power in the *passions*, in description, in the mock heroic, I leave others to descant. I take him on his strong ground as an *ethical* poet: in the former, none excel; in the mock heroic and the ethical, none equal him; and, in my mind, the latter is the highest of all poetry, because it does that in *verse*, which the greatest of men have wished to accomplish in prose. If the essence of poetry must be a *lie*, throw it to the dogs, or banish it from your republic, as Plato would have done. He who can reconcile poetry with truth and wisdom, is the only true "*poet*" in its real sense, "the *maker*", "the *creator*"—why must this mean the "liar", the "feigner", the "tale-teller"? A man may make and create better things than these.'

(LJ, v, 559)

This serves to explain Byron's passionate concern for an art which he often appeared to scorn as merely, to use a telling line from *English Bards and Scotch Reviewers* (10), 'that mighty instrument of little men'. Unless poetry held relevance to life's actualities and transcended itself into ethic, it was of secondary importance; and with Pope it had so transcended itself.

Throughout his life Byron scorned fiction and steadily laboured to attune his own genius to historical exactitude. From the start, his poetry was deeply concerned with the actual, whether through his own experiences or those of nations, with a close regard for peoples and politics and almost, we might say, a journalist's interest in historic places. His greater plays, *Marino Faliero*, *The Two Foscari* and *Sardanapalus*, were undertaken as strictly historical studies to which he devoted a close research. Writing to Murray of *Marino Faliero*, he once remarked that he hated 'things all fiction', and even found *Othello* and *The Merchant of Venice* the less satisfying on that account: 'There should always be some foundation for the most airy fabric, and pure invention is but the talent of a liar'.[1] Byron shows no

[1] 2 April, 1817; LJ, IV, 93.

explicit recognition of the sense in which Shakespeare's work was more than a decorated fiction; and in his age, since interpretative theory has been slow to evolve, this was inevitable. But what his critical mind could not be expected to recognize, his prose and poetry, with their clustering Shakespearian reminiscences and quotations, themselves witness, illustrating how closely Shakespeare was involved in his own deepest and most urgent convictions and purposes; more, his whole life, as I hope in due course to show, may be defined directly in terms of Shakespearian drama.[1] The truth is, Shakespeare, whom he regarded as 'the *worst* of models, though the most extraordinary of writers',[2] was too close to him in point of passion and energy to serve as an ideal; the ideal must be set beyond the world of Shakespearian and Byronic passion, and all those sexual and political upheavals of which such passion may be variously the cause or the reflection. What he searched for was something of classic purity. We have already seen (p. 148) how Pope's work compared to the moderns was said to bear the relation of 'a Grecian temple of the purest architecture' to a mosque. Again, writing to Moore, 3 May, 1821:

'As to Pope, I have always regarded him as the greatest name in our poetry. Depend upon it, the rest are barbarians. He is a Greek Temple, with a Gothic Cathedral on one hand, and a Turkish Mosque and all sorts of fantastic pagodas and conventicles about him. You may call Shakespeare and Milton pyramids, if you please, but I prefer the Temple of Theseus, or the Parthenon, to a mountain of burnt brick-work.'

(LJ, v, 274)

That is a neat definition. The Gothic Cathedral symbolizes medieval art, while the oriental references are exactly applicable to the poetry of romanticism, which reaches its typifying crystallization, as I have shown throughout *The Starlit Dome*, in picture-symbols of domes and other oriental structures; in *Kubla Khan* pre-eminently, but also elsewhere, with the peculiarly significant repudiation in Wordsworth's *Prelude* (VIII, 70–120). Shakespeare and Milton, being hard to place, are at least given a symbol of huge size and starry-pointing aspiration. But all this was to Byron no mere matter of artistic

[1] My study of Byron's Shakespearian relationship is nearing completion and will appear under the title *Byron and Shakespeare*.

[2] To Murray, 14 July, 1821; LJ, v, 323.

technique, or rather that and the greater realities were with him indistinguishable. The central definition of the perfect political order as 'a fair free Commonwealth' in *Marino Faliero* takes the form of a Grecian temple, whose pillars are exactly proportional to the main structure, 'giving and taking strength reciprocal' to compose the 'grace and beauty' of the whole.[1] The classic ideal was to permeate life, through and through. This meant both the full use and the perfected mastery of passion; it meant at once freedom and control; it meant poise, and it meant peace, for mankind.

We cannot too strongly emphasize that in his insistence on Pope's ethic, Byron was not supporting a conventional didacticism. Of that there was not, and never had been, in any age, a lack. We have just seen how to him 'morality' was the preserve of 'rascals'. His own life-long battle against hypocrisy and cant leaves no room for doubt here. His defence of Pope is throughout robust and broad-minded, with scant mercy shown to 'this immaculate period, this moral millenium of expurgated editions in books, manners, and royal trials of divorce'.[2] He praises *Eloisa to Abelard* for treating its subject 'with so much delicacy, mingled, at the same time, with such true and intense passion'; [3] the ethic lies in the subtlety and sympathy of the handling. As for the poem's supposed 'licentiousness':

'Licentiousness!—there is more real mischief and sapping licentiousness in a single French prose novel, in a Moravian hymn, or a German comedy, than in all the actual poetry that ever was penned or poured forth, since the rhapsodies of Orpheus. The sentimental anatomy of Rousseau and Mad^e de S. are far more formidable than any quantity of verse. They are so, because they sap the principles, by *reasoning* upon the *passions*; whereas poetry is in itself passion, and does not systematize. It assails, but does not argue; it may be wrong, but it does not assume pretensions to Optimism.'

(LJ, v, 582)

This might apply well enough to *Don Juan*. Poetry throws up the basic energies and substances for our inspection and experience, but reasoning must be used with caution. To 'reason upon the passions' may, by stating a static, superficial and specious morality ('pretensions') without contact with the vitalities, 'sap' the inmost 'principles', the vital energies, of true virtue. Poetry is largely 'passion'

[1] *Marino Faliero*, III, ii.
[2] LJ, v, 575.
[3] LJ, v, 581.

and avoids—Byron has already, in another context, said as much (p. 119)—systemization: it attacks by revealing.

So much may be said of all poetry, of the poetry Byron writes off as 'fiction', the poetry of Homer and Shakespeare. But Byron was also out to differentiate Pope as ethical poet from such great predecessors. It is, however, clear that he was being admired not for any intellectual system—Pope once himself repudiated the thought, claiming to move freely among all systems with no ultimate allegiance other than righteousness [1]—but for his passionate awareness of energies, and will to relate them through poetic expression to highest virtue. That is why Byron emphasized his supremacy in (i) the mock heroic and (ii) ethical poetry (p. 149), these two together signifying an incorporation of old energies into a new virtue. This is all very different from a simple didacticism. Pope distinguished his satiric use of real persons from 'general propositions' and 'precepts' which, being merely rational, or mental, could not be supposed to affect the 'passions', the strongest 'motive' of 'reformation'.[2] Now, though he finally achieved this peculiar excellence of ethical poetry, yet from the start his technique and diction had themselves been pointing the way. We could perhaps say that the morality of all poetry exists in its compression and pointing, through diction, rhyme, metre, or stanza, of emotional essences; and we can observe that Byron in our last quotation distinguishes poetry from the immoralities of novel and drama. It has a discipline which they lack; and yet, if it departs too far from the required technique, it becomes a vulgarity, and that is, in Byron's thinking, an immorality, the terms being to him all but identical, and hence his violent antipathy to the Cockneys. We may, indeed, recall that Pope's *Inferno*, *The Dunciad*, was not filled with seducers, murderers, or oppressors, for of those he has little to say beyond placing them snugly among the harmonies of the *Essay on Man*, but with failings more subtle and, granted a millennial view, more important: it is filled with dealers in dull, that is dead, literature.

If we transfer, point by point, the thoughts of the *Essay on Criticism* from the art of poetry to the art of life, we shall get some idea of the *poetic morality* which Pope and Byron are offering. It cannot really be defined in moral terms; it is rather a harmonization

[1] *Horace*, *Ep*. I, i, 23–34.

[2] To Arbuthnot, 26 July, 1734; quoted Tillotson, Conclusion, 163; and see p. 72 above.

of essences with a resultant poise such as that defined in Nietzsche's *Thus Spake Zarathustra*, which may, and perhaps must, be, at least in description, associated with the aristocratic, and that means the civilized, traditions of Europe, rooting back to ancient Greece. Such 'poise' is not specifically religious; instead, it will mature rather from a just balancing of religious and secular compulsions. Man's instincts are respected, even honoured; his civic and political compulsions, which may well conflict with his personal religious intuitions, have their place. The humanistic is fully involved and contained, and there is accordingly a peculiar point in the exquisite balancing of statesmanship and poetry in the following tribute to Pope's 'moral wisdom':

'If they had said nothing of *Pope*, they might have remained "alone with their glory", for aught I should have said or thought about them or their nonsense. But if they interfere with the "little Nightingale" of Twickenham, they may find others who will bear it—*I* won't. Neither time, nor distance, nor grief, nor age, can ever diminish my veneration for him, who is the great moral poet of all times, of all climes, of all feelings, and of all stages of existence. The delight of my boyhood, the study of my manhood, perhaps (if allowed to me to attain it), he may be the consolation of my age. His poetry is the Book of Life. Without canting, and yet without neglecting religion, he has assembled all that a good and great man can gather together of moral wisdom cloathed in consummate beauty. Sir William Temple observes "that of all the numbers of mankind that live within the compass of a thousand years, for one man that is born capable of making a *great poet*, there may be a *thousand* born capable of making as great generals and ministers of state as any in story". Here is a statesman's opinion of poetry: it is honourable to him, and to the art. Such a "poet of a thousand years" was *Pope*. A thousand years will roll away before such another can be hoped for in our literature. But it can *want* them—he himself is a literature.'

(LJ, v, 590)

Observe carefully our central passage:

'Without canting, and yet without neglecting religion, he has assembled all that a good and great man can gather together of moral wisdom cloathed in consummate beauty.'

Surely no sentence was ever more packed with value. Insincerity is ruled out, but religion, though it does not dictate, is nevertheless contained; the 'wisdom' has been gradually 'assembled' from a lifetime of varied experience by one who is not merely 'good', for that is not enough, but also 'great', a term hinting a full incorporation of basic energies. The phrase 'moral wisdom' itself suggests a depth beyond morality as generally received; and it is endued with poetic 'beauty', thus approaching the Greek ideal of actions not merely good, but beautiful. This is the heart of Byron's faith.

What shall we say of these remarkable passages, written by a man who consistently rated poetry as inferior to action and statesmanship? Byron despised poetry-as-fiction or poetry-as-self-expression; what he wanted was poetry-as-ethic or poetry-as-civic-power. The ethic here acclaimed is an ethic taking full count of passions and politics; it is no limited, specifically religious, didacticism, yet religion is somehow housed and contained: 'without canting, and yet without neglecting religion'. To Byron, morality was, normally, cant, and religion, if directly preached, would generally appear so too, since, as he often observed, the principles preached were lived neither by their exponents, nor by the society they upheld. Statesmanship he regularly respected, and its graceful interplay with poetry in our last passage is peculiarly interesting, each honouring the other. Because he has offered a living wisdom making no distinction of church from state, Pope's work is rated as the 'Book of Life'. We are, indeed, close to religion. Byron himself respected the Christian Church, and had an especial feeling for Catholicism; and his love for Pope was entwined with this very feeling. In opposing the rating of Cowper's *Homer* above Pope's, he wrote: 'And now that we have heard the Catholic reproached with envy, duplicity, licentiousness, avarice—what was the Calvinist?' [1] And yet the wisdom and reverence surveyed by Pope and Byron are not quite those of the Christian Church; the wisdom is an incarnate wisdom, and the reverence includes a reverence for all that is secular in human life.

Byron makes no attack on 'religion'; on the contrary, he honours and reverences it in a manner worthy of a Dr. Johnson or a T. S. Eliot; but his positive valuations are none the less a challenge. He is driven at least to *associate* Pope, 'the greatest moral poet of any age or in any language',[2] with the New Testament itself:

'The depreciation of Pope is partly founded upon a false idea of the

[1] LJ, v, 558.

[2] LJ, v, 568.

dignity of his order of poetry, to which he has partly contributed by the ingenious boast,

That not in Fancy's maze he wander'd long,
But stoop'd *to Truth, and moralized his song.*[1]

He should have written "rose to truth". In my mind, the highest of all poetry is ethical poetry, as the highest of all earthly objects must be moral truth. Religion does not make a part of my subject; it is something beyond human powers, and has failed in all human hands except Milton's and Dante's, and even Dante's powers are involved in his delineation of human passions, though in supernatural circumstances. What made Socrates the greatest of men? His moral truth —his ethics. What proved Jesus Christ the Son of God hardly less than his miracles? His moral precepts. And if ethics have made a philosopher the first of men, and have not been disdained as an adjunct to his Gospel by the Deity himself, are we to be told that ethical poetry, or didactic poetry, or by whatever name you term it, whose object is to make men better and wiser, is not the *very first order* of poetry; and are we to be told this too by one of the priesthood? It requires more mind, more wisdom, more power, than all the "forests" that ever were "walked for their description", and all the epics that ever were founded upon fields of battle. The *Georgics* are indisputably, and, I believe, *undisputedly*, even a finer poem than the *Aeneid*. Virgil knew this; he did not order *them* to be burnt:

The proper study of Mankind is Man.[2]

'It is the fashion of the day to lay great stress upon what they call "imagination" and "invention", the two commonest of qualities: an Irish peasant with a little whisky in his head will imagine and invent more than would furnish forth a modern poem. If Lucretius had not been spoiled by the Epicurean system, we should have had a far superior poem to any now in existence. As mere poetry, it is the first of Latin poems. What then has ruined it? His ethics. Pope has not this defect; his moral is as pure as his poetry is glorious.'

(v, 554)

[1] *Epistle to Dr. Arbuthnot*, 340.
[2] *Essay on Man*, II, 2.

Our warning must be repeated: Byron's use of the word 'precepts' must not mislead us. The New Testament does not, strictly speaking, offer 'precepts' at all; its two positive commandments are vague and general; its teaching is illustrated mainly through parable, or poetry, and so felt as an outflowering from life itself; the righteousness of the Pharisees is repudiated; and Christ himself is, not the preceptor, but 'the way'. All this, of course, Byron knew well enough, though the phrasing of it in a pre-Nietzschean era was perhaps impossible. What held him in both the New Testament and in Pope was less a doctrine than a power, the power St. Paul spoke of, for good; the poetry of the *Essay on Man*, *Moral Essays* and *Imitations of Horace* being less an obvious teaching than a diagnosis of falsities and doctrine of sublimation, aiming to set 'the *Passions* on the side of Truth',[1] with a will to human and social wholeness, or integrity. Byron admired Pope for his Nietzschean affinities, and it is because he found in Pope this higher teaching, which was to flower so purely in *Thus Spake Zarathustra*, that he was warmed by him as by no other writer of modern times.

IV

Pope as a poet of peace follows Shakespeare and Milton rather as the New Testament follows the old. In both the earlier conflicts are incorporated; the relation of Pope to Shakespeare is often exact (pp. 43–6), and the conflict of religion and humanism in Milton is, with comparatively little left out, resolved in Pope. In both the New Testament and Pope we find a certain quiescence, at least as far as outward action is concerned, with a new emphasis on personal, and in Pope civic, regeneration. The old conflicts are resolved not by any static proposition or propositions, but by a living incarnation, in the 'here' and 'now': what could not be thought out, is lived into. More, in both there is a transference from a limited nationalism, for Shakespeare and Milton were nationalist poets or prophets as surely as the writers of the Old Testament, to an emphasis on (i) the individual, and (ii) the greater whole, or God. So Pope, who, unlike the New Testament, includes also the civic, political, and aristocratic virtues, is really less national than specifically, as was Byron later, international, with an internationalism which may be said to reflect the political implications of St. Paul's epistles.

[1] *Horace, Ep.* II, i, 218.

Byron's phrase 'the Christianity of English poetry' (p. 132) should be carefully studied. 'Literature', or 'poetry', contains, as divine inspiration does not, a human element; that is, it is in part secular; it surveys and incorporates the animal energies and the political energies; in it body and soul, state and church, may be felt in conflict or in resolution, but at least they are both there. The New Testament, as we are taught to understand it, does not directly survey this territory, except by off-hand comment; it represents the delivery of a great, perhaps the greatest, message man has ever received *under conditions of immediate stability assured by the secular rule of Rome*. Its descendant, the Christian Church, has existed beside, and often in tension with, the secular state. But poetry in the Renaissance world has steadily tried to assimilate the one to the other. Dante was on the side of Emperor as against Pope, and his great vision was a vision of world-order centred in Rome. Poets from Aeschylus, Sophocles and Virgil to Wordsworth, Tennyson and Francis Berry aim to sanctify the secular and secularize, without diluting, the sacred; or may sometimes, as are Hardy and Eliot, be found expressing a sense of acute discomfort at what appears a final incompatibility. You can therefore see why Byron, who of all great poets was most deeply involved in matters national, political, and international, was drawn to Pope instead of to the New Testament. If you look through his works, prose and poetry, you will find very few references to Christ, but you will find continual evidence that he was saturated, as poet, thinker, and in the widest sense as man, in the Old Testament. The two books he loved best throughout his life were, without any question, the Old Testament and the works of Pope; the one completed the other; he was personally drawn less to the Prince of Peace than to the Poet of Peace; and that is why he called Pope 'the Christianity of English poetry'.

We have heard, in our time, much about 'tradition'. But there are two main traditions for us to consider. There is the tradition descending from medieval Christianity and the Church of Rome, through the more specifically religious implications of Dante and the more medieval aspects of Shakespeare to the prose and poetry of the seventeenth century; and thence to the Dantesque affinities of Byron, and on to T. S. Eliot. But there is also the other, more humanist, and dramatic, tradition, descending from ancient Greece, through Virgil and Dante as prophets of world-order, to Renaissance Italy and Shakespeare, to Pope and Byron; and thence to Ibsen, Nietzsche, and Bernard Shaw.[1] Both have their rights, and both can today claim to serve the cause of the New Testament, of Christ Himself. And, though we can, surely, agree that the desired end is a synthesis, disagreement will necessarily arise as soon as we start talking of the future, since each will clearly assert that it has room for the other, if only it be allowed to guide. We in England are always ready to be shocked at any suggestion of Crown rather than Church as prime mediator between Christ and man, too often forgetting that its connotations far outspace the secular, and that it still remains, in our national body, supreme.

Byron's ranging imagination was not limited to a secular humanism, but could imagine Italy, or Rome, as both 'Mother of Arts' and

Parent of our religion! whom the wide
Nations have knelt to for the keys of Heaven!
(*Childe Harold*, IV, 47)

He could, through the person of Dante, survey St. Peter's as

a fane surpassing all before,
Such as all flesh shall flock to kneel in: ne'er
Such sight hath been unfolded by a door
As this, to which all nations shall repair,
And lay their sins at this huge gate of Heaven.
(*The Prophecy of Dante*, IV)

As man, poet, and thinker, Byron really covers both traditions, as did Dante [2] and Shakespeare; and that is why the word 'nations' recurs when he thinks of Rome: the sins are the sins, not of individuals, but of nations. Byron is our pivot; looking back to the ancients, Dante, Shakespeare and Pope, he is also the precursor of Ibsen and Nietzsche, those great dramatic thinkers who were tormented by knowledge of the pressing need to achieve a new harmony of Church and State. The bonds of civilization were bursting asunder. Byron had felt it coming; much, in the French Revolution, had already come. Religion, as Europe knows it, is not enough. So he, Ibsen and Nietzsche, all three looked back to the

[1] I am thinking of *Emperor and Galilean* (*Christ and Nietzsche*, II, 56, 65–7; V, 216, and note; VI, 235, 237), and Shaw's deep concern with the psychology of government; e.g. in *Caesar and Cleopatra* and *Back to Methuselah*.

[2] A good account of Dante as political prophet and of his relation to Byron may be found in Joseph Mazzini's essays *On the Minor Works of Dante* and *Byron and Goethe*.

ancient world; each tried to preserve the best of the Renaissance and aristocratic values; each had dreams of a greater humanity to be; each after his own fashion laboured to bring Church and State together. The task was bitter: each in turn had to shock those who thought contemporary Christianity was a real religion; each fought against cant and was accused of devilish wickedness; and we need not deny that, with his blinding clarity of sight, and his greater experience of the developing disruption, Nietzsche was led to speak out, at times, 'not wisely, but too well'. But what would we have? Do not our quotations from Byron in this essay themselves, in all their riot and wealth, witness the growing complexity, the inroads of chaos? Those who carried the torch yet deeper into the night of the great 'anarch' whose advent Pope had foreseen at the conclusion to *The Dunciad*, carried it through buffeting winds. It was often near enough, as it is today, to extinction; and whenever it flares momentarily in the darkness, it gilds its bearer's face with a satanic hue. But it remains our torch, our beacon, none the less; and it will be fatal to leave that truth unrecognized.

To compose the great conflicts tearing our world we cannot remain content with secular politics. But neither can we expect our Church, as a Church, to guide, or lead; in matters psychological, social or political, it shows no sign of being able or willing to attempt such a task; it acts as a leaven, as an auxiliary, in no sense a master. And it is perhaps right that it should do so. We do not really want a new religion; what we want is something for which we have no name, something forecast by Nietzsche's intuition of a 'Roman Caesar with the soul of Christ',[1] the 'third empire' of Ibsen's *Emperor and Galilean*, in which Church and State will have been dissolved, with, nevertheless, victory for neither, and fullest blessings maintained of both; in which each will indeed be themselves for the first time in history within what Tennyson foresaw as those 'new majesties of mighty states',[2] that 'Parliament of man' and 'Federation of the world'[3] to be ushered in by the new nobility of those greater men who are to compose 'the Christ that is to be'.[4]

It cannot be exactly defined; it is for us, for our world, to create the definition.[5] But to Byron at least it was forecast by the life-work

[1] *The Will to Power*, IV, vi, 983.
[2] *Love Thou Thy Land.*
[3] *Locksley Hall.*
[4] *In Memoriam*, CVI.
[5] We seem already to be trying to do so; and our interest in the poetic styles of Shakespeare and Donne can be related to the attempt. In *The Shakespearean*

of Pope as a, or rather *the*, universal poet, of mankind, of peace. Pope, a Catholic by upbringing, was in effect a deist (p. 6 above); Byron, whose explicit religious beliefs were deistic, was imaginatively drawn to Catholicism; but for neither could any religion, as such, exist apart from that greater catholicism, including all basic energies and all political purposes, to which their lives were similarly dedicated.[1] The politics were more than national. Byron, banished by ostracism from his native land, could the more naturally take a cosmopolitan, an international, view. He writes home from Italy to England as to a nation of strangers, unwilling to insult their national idols:

'I shall not presume to say that Pope is as high a poet as Shakespeare and Milton, though his enemy, Warton, places him immediately under them. I would no more say this than I would assert in the mosque (once Saint Sophia's), that Socrates was a greater than Mahomet.'

(LJ, v, 560)

But, he says,

'If any great national or natural convulsion could or should overwhelm your country in such sort as to sweep Great Britain from the kingdoms of the earth, and leave only that, after all, the most living of human things, a *dead language*, to be studied and read, and imitated, by the wise of future and far generations, upon foreign shores; if your literature should become the learning of mankind, divested of party cabals, temporary fashions, and national pride and prejudice; —an Englishman, anxious that the posterity of strangers should know that there had been such a thing as a British Epic and Tragedy, might wish for the preservation of Shakespeare and Milton; but the surviving World would snatch Pope from the wreck, and let the rest sink with the people. He is the moral poet of all civilization; and as such, let us hope that he will one day be the national poet of mankind.'

(LJ, v, 560)

Moment (1954) Patrick Cruttwell has recently defined the social *milieu* of the early seventeenth century as a society trying to realize in England the medieval dream of Emperor and Pope in unison (IV, 109). See my review of Mr. Cruttwell's book in *The Universities Quarterly*, Aug., 1954; 401.

[1] For a more precise relation of Pope's doctrine to 'religion' see p. 178 below.

We are not ourselves making these claims for Pope; we are merely expounding Byron's views. His phrases make an amazing cluster: 'the greatest moral poet of any age or in any language' (p. 143), the 'poet of a thousand years' (p. 153), 'himself a literature' (p. 153), the 'Christianity of English poetry' (p. 132) and 'Book of Life' (p. 153); and now, 'the moral poet of all civilization' and 'national poet of mankind'. With these phrases, it is true, we need not agree, but, even so, we shall not forget them. For whether or not they be true of Pope is of less importance than *the reasons that led Byron to make them.*

We may well ask—has not Byron's own poetic universe a richness and variety, a dimension of action, far in excess of Pope's? And can we agree that all this is outweighed by Pope's perfection of execution and precision of ethical psychology? Surely Byron's emphasis on the supremity of poetic doctrine, which is *not* the doctrine of intellectual ethics, has its limitations? Yes. But only for one reason. Pope's universe, in its way perfect, is yet the reflection of a single class in one nation at a certain point of time; and even so, much polished for the purpose, and indeed itself an attack on contemporary society for its unrealized virtue. It reflects a peaceful society; it speaks in terms of the arts and the compulsions of peace, its sweetness and its dangers; but such peace, to us, can only be known in a limited context. Byron's world is far greater; nor is it peaceful; it is a world labouring for peace. If ever a perfect world-order is established on earth, then perhaps such works as *Marino Faliero* and *Sardanapalus* may grow out of date. We cannot say, and the discussion is perhaps profitless. But, were they to do so, we may yet suggest that the New Testament itself and *Thus Spake Zarathustra* would still be confronting man with a spiritual challenge; and, with them, the works of Pope. What Shakespeare did for Elizabethan England and Pope for Augustan London, Byron attempted for Europe, for the world. And he was right in taking the spiritualized humanism of Pope for his exemplar. Byron willed the good, not of Britain alone, but of all mankind, as one family; one brotherhood; and of that family, that brotherhood, Pope, the poet of peace *par excellence*, and therefore the chastiser of *the vices of peace*, is the star. But the works of Shakespeare and Byron, perhaps of many Shakespeares and many Byrons, must be lived through before the culture of Augustan aristocracy as sublimated and purified almost out of recognition by the genius of Pope becomes the universal lot of mankind.

V

AFTERTHOUGHTS

V. AFTERTHOUGHTS

PEACE is no idle business, for energies are the stuff of life. Pope is clearly not a poet of conflict and war, as are Shakespeare, Milton and, with reservations, since his work is pointed, even more explicitly than Shakespeare's, towards peace, Byron; but his world is tinglingly alive and active. Its aim is the just ordering of energies in man and society. Balanced opposition replaces conflict to compose a harmony which becomes ethic. He seems to say, as did Castiglione before him and Nietzsche's Zarathustra after, that best action can only mature from a blend of energy with form to make the supreme 'way' and only living virtue.

Pope's early poetic instincts were pastoral, his *Pastorals* being published in 1709 and the *Messiah* in 1712. Such a start marks in itself no lack of energy or purpose. For what *is* pastoral? Pastoral normally envisages man in a sunny climate at work which appears to be limited to the comparatively easy business of guarding and caring for one's flock: life is, or appears, simple. But is this necessarily a release? No. For now we are faced only the more clearly by the basic torments of life: love and death, unreachable desire and irreparable loss. The pastoral—you feel it in Lyly's plays—defines the problems and tensions awaiting man when, if ever, all other turmoils are stilled. Of Pope's four early pastorals, the two best, Summer and Winter, are concerned respectively with love and death. Here is the conclusion to *Summer*:

But see, the shepherds shun the noonday heat,
The lowing herds to murm'ring brooks retreat,
To closer shades the panting flocks remove;
Ye Gods! and is there no relief for Love?

But soon the sun with milder rays descends
To the cool ocean, where his journey ends.
On me love's fiercer flames for ever prey,
By night he scorches, as he burns by day.

(85)

In poetry of a nearly equal poignancy *Winter* mourns the loss of a loved one, with exquisite references of human death to nature's winter:

Behold the groves that shine with silver frost,
Their beauty wither'd, and their verdure lost . . .

(9)

The poetry would relate the human wound to natural process, and so integrate man's soul into his natural setting. Hence the contrast in our first passage of nature's kindly rhythms with man's enduring pain; the very contrast grows from the will towards its surmounting.

Nature is one solution; poetry the other. In pastoral there is not only the obvious poetry. The *dramatis personae* are themselves poets, and engage in poetic competitions. In balancing man against nature, love against death, season with season, in the antiphonal speeches of the persons, and the technique of the poetry itself, in all this we can say that pastoral is attempting to create a balance, or poise, in despite of, indeed composed of, man's most ultimate pains and problems. It holds, in small compass, the essentials of all literary composition.

It is, moreover, clear, as E. K. Chambers long ago pointed out in an admirable essay,[1] that the English pastoral tradition descending from Theocritus and Virgil blends, as in *Lycidas*, with the religious pastoralism descending from the Old and New Testaments and incorporated into the Christian church (e.g. David as shepherd-boy, the shepherds visited by the Angel of the Lord, such phrases as 'feed my sheep' and 'the good shepherd', the Bishop's crook, the word 'pastor'). The two are necessarily akin, since pastoral suggests peace, and Christianity worships the Prince of Peace. It is not, therefore, surprising that Pope should have composed a poem called *Messiah* (1712) blending the prophecy of Isaiah with Virgil's Messianic Eclogue, which he took to derive, through the Sibylline books, from the Hebrew. In the *Messiah* a golden age is prophesied. The Saviour

[1] *English Pastorals*, Introduction to Selections (no date).

crushes Death and Hell and tends man as a loving 'shepherd'. Wars are gone:

No more shall nation against nation rise,
Nor ardent warriors meet with hateful eyes,
Nor fields with gleaming steel be cover'd o'er,
The brazen trumpets kindle rage no more.

(57)

All nature is transmuted, while 'boys in flow'ry bands the tiger lead' (78), a pretty image of what Pope is always himself doing, as, with his exquisite harmonies, he tames and guides man's tigerish passions.

Such is the soil from which *Windsor Forest* (1713), *The Rape of the Lock* (1712–14), *Eloisa to Abelard* (1717), and the *Elegy to the Memory of an Unfortunate Lady* (1717), grow. Before passing on, a word or two on these may be offered: they are poems respectively of (i) pastoral peace, (ii) aristocratic society, (iii) unsatisfied love and (iv) death. All spring from the pastoral.

Of *Windsor Forest* we have treated already. In its completed, 1713, form, it develops a neat reference of idyllic pastoral to Britain, and of Britain to peace. The first *Pastorals* with their references to Windsor and the Cam were careful to keep contemporary Britain in mind; here those gestures are expanded. Britain is regarded as the enemy of oppression, and peace invoked by Father Thames:

Hail, sacred peace! hail, long-expected days,
That Thames's glory to the stars shall raise!
Tho' Tiber's streams immortal Rome behold,
Tho' foaming Hermus swells with tides of gold,
From heav'n itself though sev'n-fold Nilus flows,
And harvests on a hundred realms bestows;
These now no more shall be the Muse's themes,
Lost in my fame, as in the sea their streams.
Let Volga's banks with iron squadrons shine,
And groves of lances glitter on the Rhine,
Let barb'rous Ganges arm a servile train;
Be mine the blessings of a peaceful reign.

(355)

Observe Pope's antipathy to '*iron* squadrons', an impression in direct descent from the '*brazen* trumpets' of his *Messiah*: he is by nature hostile to such metallic and Miltonic impressions. Noble or sacred structures are of a different category, so 'Temples rise, the beauteous works of Peace', and London is crowned by 'a new Whitehall' (378–80). For the rest, the poem's main emphasis falls on nature and the softer emotions, and he would like these to involve each other. It is 'Albion's', or Britain's, task to assure that happy consummation.[1]

Next, *The Rape of the Lock*, which belongs here more precisely than may at first appear. Its setting is society, its theme a social quarrel, its moral, the futility of ill-temper. An aristocratic and peaceful society is assumed, and wars, politics, and social injustice not really relevant, as may appear from the jarring nature of the couplet:

The hungry Judges soon the sentence sign,
And wretches hang that jurymen may dine.

(III, 21)

The satiric point is in itself worth making, but its implications so appallingly awful that it rings discordant in the context and risks shattering our poem. Neither here nor even in his later satires is Pope opposing such obvious wrongs; he speaks normally only of the subtler evils of an aristocratic society in full enjoyment of place and peace, of man removed, as in pastoral poetry, from natural hardship, strenuous labour, and social unrest. The aristocratic *milieu* of the last few centuries corresponds directly to the pastoral, and that is why we find so many pastoral, or otherwise Greek mythological, elements in the interior decorations and templed gardens, such as those at Stowe, of the aristocracy of Pope's day.

Of *Eloisa to Abelard* little more need be said: it is a full dramatic exploitation of the love-torment less powerfully present in pastoral, and here most beautifully balanced with divine love. The poem's statement is in the careful weighing and balancing, not just in the conclusion, and it recalls the balancing of human and divine love and beauty in Spenser's four *Hymns*: both Lyly and Spenser write from a world-view close to Pope's. With *Eloisa to Abelard* we may group the *Elegy to the Memory of an Unfortunate Lady*, a poem of considerable pathos and power, offering a fine treatment of unrestful ambition as 'the glorious fault of Angels and of Gods' (14), balanced against a denunciation of 'steel'd' sympathies, unyielding hearts, and

[1] See also my short essay on Pope entitled 'The New Whitehall' in *Hiroshima* (1946).

the short-lived and brittle pageantry of the mighty 'proud', and concluding:

> *So perish all, whose breast ne'er learn'd to glow*
> *For others good, or melt at others woe.*
>
> (41–6)

This is our first sample of that satiric anger that is to burn so powerfully later. Patriotism is constituent to the emphasized pathos of the lady's death abroad, and among foreigners. The only comfort is in nature, idyllically presented.

There is clearly nothing placid about Pope. As his work develops it becomes vitriolic in attack, but the attack, like that of the New Testament or *Thus Spake Zarathustra*, which both presuppose a peaceful society, is levelled less against obvious wrong-doing than against the subtler evils of insincerity, false reason, mentalized education, pride, avarice, and ambition. On the other side, his positives are instinct, the voice of God, nature, kindness to men and animals, peace, the cosmic whole. His final purpose is to set 'the Passions on the side of Truth'; [1] to deliver morality from her 'false guardians'; [2] to establish, as Byron saw (p. 153), a virtue which is not cant; and to charge with a newly enlightened significance the traditional values of patriotism and fame. Death and love are, it is true, not emphasized in his later work, but Pope's function as a poet of peace may be said to fall in line with his pastoral beginnings.

The 'campaign of peace' is naturally strenuous, since, the more obvious outlets of competition removed, man is thrown back on himself and endures the severest of all possible tests. He cannot remain static. He is, whether we like it or not, a dynamo; and he is this for a purpose which, in its turn, cannot be understood without due regard to his dynamic nature. That is the subject of the *Essay on Man*.

This crowning work has already been discussed. Here I would merely add a few afterthoughts. The interpretation already given provides a peculiarly interesting example of 'spatial' analysis. The *Essay on Man* is certainly philosophic, and yet its meaning can only be understood in terms of its artistic structure; it is, in its own way, one of our 'musical buildings'. Fundamental to all religion, art and philosophy lies the all but insoluble problem of assimilating the world of good and evil in man's experience to the divine powers.

[1] *Horace, Ep.* II, i, 218.

[2] *Dunciad*, IV, 27.

In the *Essay on Man* we have various epistles with their own, water-tight, approaches, at least two apparently incompatible philosophies being presented in balance, and yet we are not asked to choose one and reject the other, but rather to accept both, and build from them a new totality. The coherence is less logical than structural, though within the structure itself can be discovered, as we have seen (pp. 51–53, 82), the inmost secret of creative living, of virtue not merely in the moral, but also in the magical, sense of that time-honoured word. Once again we find Pope working with balance, since by using both of the two main life-views possible, he outlines a 'way' towards equipoise and harmony. We can thus watch the 'spatial' approach doing what logic could not do, and perhaps in no other work on record is its nature so clear; so that study of the *Essay* assists our understanding of the spatial, or rather space-time, nature of art in general. It is a grand-style example of the truth that a poet does not so much think thoughts as *make* them, though it may be for us to attempt to think the thoughts which he has made. As in a drama, where truth is shadowed by conflicting voices, so the *Essay* builds from opposition a unity. Christian symbolism is directly comparable. The Trinity itself is a sublime paradox involving dramatic interactivity within a triangular unity; and to understand it you have, in the mind's eye, to give it spatial formulation, since without such a triangular image you can scarcely receive the resolution of Three-in-One and One-in-Three.

Though such an approach, based, as all sound interpretation must be, on the space-time nature of art, what had for generations been regarded as the second-hand versification of a second-rate philosophy took on significance as doctrine.[1] Once again, the old type of 'source' had been silenced. Scholars no longer limit the meaning of *Antony and Cleopatra* by consideration of Plutarch, nor will they in future regard Pope's *Essay on Man* as a pastiche of Bolingbrokian metaphysics; and in any case, as Carl van Doren remarked to me many years ago, the main substances of Pope's poem are not to be found in Bolingbroke. We must hope that, the ground now cleared, there will

[1] The nature of my divergence from the traditional reading will be clear from Geoffrey Tillotson's remark: 'Pope was at his weakest as a philosopher. The *Essay on Man* is beautifully planned on paper, but not as reason' ('Design', 48). My whole point is, that the planning, or structure, *is* the philosophy; and that by such a dynamic, or dramatic, method, Pope has come near to solving the enigma of good and evil.

not be any return, as in Shakespeare there has been, to an over-concentration on contemporary philosophies of 'order' to the neglect of the central achievement. After all, the philosophies concerned are, in both instances, the vast and general philosophies of order, hierarchy, and harmony. Such conceptions are not the preserve of any particular age or culture, though each in turn will naturally shape and colour them to taste: you find them variously in Indian, Greek, Medieval and Renaissance thought; and among the Incas of Peru. That admitted, what we have to do is to study not the official philosophies, but what our poet or dramatist does with them. The danger is more insidious than it at first appears, since there is always a tendency to weigh down the winged poetry, to clog its wings, with, to use Pope's impolite phrase, such 'learned lumber'.[1] We must sternly avoid the temptation to explain poetry in terms of secondary rather than final causes, to regard it as something rooted backward rather than as something pointing on. For it cannot endure enslavement to any static scheme, however vast; it is a living organism, and as such must be understood. Our interpretative discoveries came not from learning, but from a plain inspection of the poetry of Shakespeare, Pope and others, and a reading of them 'with the same spirit'—and that means, as F. W. Bateson has reminded us, with the same vital and creative insight—'that its author writ'.[2]

Such was the reading of *The Essay on Man* first given in 'The Vital Flame' (1939) and, there is little doubt that it has come to stay. In his introduction to the fine *Twickenham* edition of the poem published in 1950, Professor Maynard Mack has followed this interpretation in accepting the 'conflict' of opposing philosophies as constituent to a dramatic whole transcending the separate approaches (lxxiii); agreeing that, though 'the presence of such ambivalences' supplies 'no answer to the logical problem', it nevertheless 'suggests that psychologically the combination of acceptance as a state of mind with moral effort as a rule of conduct is both possible and sound' (xlvi); and that poetry, while refusing judgement on the plane of logic, can 'take the argument to another plane altogether', where the problem is 'dissolved' in an 'enlarged' context (lxx). He, too, both observes Pope's Shakespearian affinities, and contrasts, in point of depth, his philosophic drama with the personified ritual-drama of Milton's Satan (see p. 48, note). Throughout he follows our spatial

[1] *Essay on Criticism*, 613.

[2] Ibid., 234.

interpretation, getting the 'meaning' (lxx) not from the parts, but from their interaction within the dramatic whole, and so restating our central doctrine that man, through trust in the creation as harmony, may 'both support and help to realize' that harmony by 'disciplining' himself (lxxx). That is, man creates (p. 50) the harmony from faith in which his creation of it develops: the doctrine is statically paradoxical but dynamically coherent, and must be understood not within the factual, but within the actual; as a living, forward-thrusting, act in a living universe.

This is what the *Essay on Man*, as an artistic whole, says; what Byron intuitively recognized, and our interpretation first clearly revealed and formulated; and on it Professor Mack has now set the seal of his acceptance in the standard edition of the poem. We can accordingly regard this interpretation as established; and that being so, we must not be surprised to find its challenge still radiating lines of force, today. Which leads us on.

Since my first interpretation, my admiration of the *Essay on Man* has been, if anything, increased. Its relevance to other works of poetic or religious doctrine appears the greater the more closely you study it, and I would urge that the opinions here expressed be read in conjunction with their further developments in my references to the *Essay* throughout *Christ and Nietzsche*. The comparison with Nietzsche must be driven home again and again:

> *The surest Virtues thus from Passions shoot,*
> *Wild Nature's vigor working at the root.*
>
> (II, 183)

The doctrine is, in fact, the doctrine of modern psychology, and whenever we feel doubtful regarding the rights of instinct, we should remember that what we call 'sublimation' cannot be accomplished without establishing a friendly relation with the thing to be sublimated, any more than you can successfully civilize a child or train an animal without love. Sublimation in direct contact with the dynamic energies may clearly be called the core of the *Essay's* doctrine, as it is also of *Thus Spake Zarathustra*. In both we are concerned with the gradual transmutation of what is, in any case, right[1] to what is, all things considered, best. The 'best' is to be inwardly experienced and inwardly recognized, and it is the only

[1] 'Whatever is, is right'; I, 294.

true happiness, as Pope reminds us when *returning to the phrase* in Book IV:

> *Whatever is, is right—This world, 'tis true,*
> *Was made for Caesar—but for Titus too:*
> *And which more blest? who chain'd his country, say,*
> *Or he whose Virtue sigh'd to lose a day?*
>
> (IV, 145)

The true virtue will not, however, be limited to a conventional morality. We are reminded of St. Paul's balancing of permission and expedience.

Though the good-and-evil antimony is, in the main, settled by the doctrine of creative psychology whereby every vice holds potentially a corresponding virtue (II, 185–94), Pope nevertheless uses also the more general thought of the two principles necessarily intershifting in every man (II, 231). Though firmly distinguishing vice from virtue (II, 211–12) and indeed regarding it as a 'monster' only to be seen to be hated (II, 217), he knows that in actual experience we find the two inextricably intertwisted and combining in 'a thousand ways' (II, 214). We have accordingly to recognize the presence of such 'extremes' joining in man 'to some mysterious use' (II, 206); we have to accept the mystery without what Byron calls 'cant' (p. 153); and somehow from this Shakespearian acceptance, this balancing of the positive and the negative within us, good matures through the grace of what Pope calls a 'mightier Pow'r' (II, 165), functioning as the 'Eternal Art' (II, 175).

That the *Essay on Man* outspaces its 'Augustan' period as normally understood we have sufficiently shown, but we need not limit its contacts to the Renaissance, widely considered, nor even to the Western tradition. In reading Sri Aurobindo's colossal work of mystical philosophy, *The Life Divine* (Calcutta, 1939), I was continually struck to find how much of his visionary structure was covered by the lucid couplets and fourfold plan of Pope's *Essay*.

I shall now intentionally select for comparison works superficially unlike Pope's *Essay*. Our obvious modern comparison would be that profound poem, so similar in scope and purpose (e.g. especially, on nature at the root of both crude instinct and spiritual illumination, III, 975–1057), Robert Bridges' *Testament of Beauty*; or that remarkable work of poetic philosophy and creative doctrine, whose very title hints its relevance to our story, Murray Hickey Ley's *A is All*

(San Francisco, 1953). Here I can only point to the many references to Bridges throughout my *Christ and Nietzsche*, and pass on to a recent work at first sight, in its wild Dionysian extravagance, the polar opposite of all that Pope, as artist, appears to stand for. I refer to John Custance's highly suggestive *Wisdom, Madness and Folly* (1951). Strange though it may seem, this work continually recalls Pope's scheme. But it is not quite so fantastic as it at first appears. Though strongly inspirational in origin, it is well-buttressed by references to thinkers of status from Kant onwards, such as Herbert Spencer, William James, Freud, Jung, Bergson, D. H. Lawrence, Berdyaev and Toynbee. Most important of all, its two basic principles, which the author calls 'negative' and 'positive', are, as he himself reminds us, roughly correspondent to Nietzsche's 'Dionysian' and 'Apollonian'. Often he calls them 'instinct' and 'reason', like Pope; and, like Pope, refers to the great 'all' or 'whole' as his final reference. Custance's positive principle, 'reason', recalls those thinkers characterized by Pope as 'more studious to divide than to unite' (II, 82); it is a faculty 'whose very nature' it is 'to divide and cut off' (V, 146); 'a male, aggressive power' with, as phallic symbol, 'a flaming sword for analysis, division, destruction' (VI, 170).[1] But its era of supremacy is coming to an end, since 'the Negative is preparing a terrible revenge on modern civilization' (IV, 93), as Pope foresaw in his vision of our disrupted culture at the close of *The Dunciad* (p. 64). Somehow the lost 'balance' must be redressed 'through a victory of the Negative', the more female, Dionysian principle, 'after its long eclipse' (V, 147). The final aim is, however, no violent orgy of visions and emotions, but a just balance, 'reconciling the opposites and allowing power to flow freely and harmoniously' (IV, 97). This is what John Custance envisages as the 'brave new world', to use Aldous Huxley's Shakespearian adaptation, ahead of us, a reconciliation which he finds complete in (i) the personality of Jesus (IV, 97) and (ii) the culture of ancient Greece, his balance recalling Byron's view of Pope as 'the Christianity of English poetry' (p. 132):

'Again and again visions of Greece appeared to me, little though I knew of the classics and classical civilization. And always the Greeks

[1] This is roughly what 'reason' meant for Pope. To Milton 'reason' was the supreme faculty, the difference being in part a difference in doctrine and in part a shift in the word's meaning.

appeared to me quite unique. They alone of all peoples had achieved a Golden Mean between Positive and Negative, and it was to this perfect balance that their amazing achievements appeared to me to be due. In charts I drew at the time attempting to classify the peoples of history according to the Positive and Negative elements, the Greeks always came along a central line. Through the Golden Mean the Kingdom of God had very nearly been created on earth.'

(IV, 97)

That is, too, Nietzsche's reading of classical culture as, at its best, a fusion of Dionysian and Apollonian. Our quotation helps us to see why Byron so admired the 'Grecian temple' (pp. 148, 150) of Pope's poetry; his was an age of Dionysian upsurgings in literature and the challenge of the masses, and of a false Apollonianism in morals and religion; his own life was one long endeavour to harmonize his tumultuous passions with an ingrained, almost puritanical, moral idealism; and he saw in Pope's exquisite Apollonian projection of a Dionysian philosophy, and there alone, since Shakespeare was *too* Dionysian, the very fusion for which he longed. We can see, too, why Pope himself drew sustenance from the ancients, his very style recapturing in balance and poise the statue-poses of antiquity (pp. 91–2). But such thoughts do not leave us on the plane of 'psychology'; those very poses enjoy and transmit a breath of the eternal; and Custance writes throughout from a sense of the eternal categories.

His graded hierarchies make a delightful list:

'There are thus, I am impelled to postulate, positive and negative Gods, or Powers of God, positive and negative saints and martyrs, angels and archangels, godesses, devils, warlocks and witches, sirens, fauns, nymphs, sprites, gnomes, gremlins, poltergeists, fairies, ghosts, men and women, anthropoids and animals, birds and insects, fishes, reptiles and bacteria.'

(VI, 167)

'Negative' here holds no suggestion of 'evil'; indeed, it is for the negative that the author is arguing. But see how closely the intuition fits Pope's natural and divine hierarchies. So too, with 'chance': in Pope's purposeful universe 'chance' is directly equated with 'direction' (I, 290; p. 46), and Custance has a similar intuition, or sense, of 'guidance' (V, 142), devoting a whole section to 'Purpose and Chance' (VI, 160–8), quoting C. S. Myers' statement that 'accidents' are 'scientific impossibilities' (VI, 163), and constructing a neat myth to illustrate a possible blending of the powers of prayer with the rights of that natural law and cosmic balance on which Pope similarly insists.[1] The practical necessity Custance finds of dividing 'the personal and purposive aspect of things up into concepts of various Beings, endowed with personality and purpose, and fulfilling various functions' (VI, 163), may be compared with the impulse, in Pope and others, towards what is technically called 'personification'. The author of *Wisdom, Madness, and Folly* is one with Nietzsche, though here Pope offers no analogy, in looking for some sort of 'superman' (VI, 182).

This is a strikingly original book, but much of it is contained, and nearly all foreshadowed, in the lucid couplets of Pope's short *Essay*. Such thinking from the heart of life will always be original, but seldom new, and needs in every age driving home against the static concepts and lifeless clichés that pass for exact thought. Or again, we may say that it is, for the most part, just common-sense. If, says Mr. Custance, he could put into words what he has seen in periods of ecstasy, he would have gone near to solving the problem of the universe. Such a statement would be of general use:

'It would give everybody a logical, intelligible and satisfactory way of life for this world and the next. It would be an indispensable *vade mecum* for every sensible person.'

(VI, 150)

It would not be unreasonable to claim as much for the *Essay on Man:* I actually did so in my original essay (p. 46 above). All this Pope knew, and underlined the thought by composing his *Universal Prayer*.

The main purpose of both is to integrate man self-consciously into a vital, purposeful, and not less than personal, universe. Above all, vitality must be assured; and this involves a full assimilation of the Dionysian. Dionysus was an oriental god. *Thus Spake Zarathustra* uses an oriental setting, and our Renaissance poets may often be supposed as labouring to incorporate a more eastern, feminine and Dionysian, at once vital and spiritual, wisdom into the more masculine and mentalized culture of the West.[2] Pope's *Essay* lies within this movement, and its affinities to Aurobindo's *Life Divine* need not surprise us. Or we may turn to another great seer of our

[1] VI, 161–2; *Essay on Man*, IV, 111–30.

[2] The relevant references are given in my *Christ and Nietzsche*, IV, 138–9.

day, at first sight poles apart from Pope, John Cowper Powys. Here he is, writing, in one of the truly great pieces of contemporary criticism and perhaps *the* greatest analysis of humour in existence, on Rabelais:

'Now the way Rabelais opens up the path in which, for one reader at least, he is, after his favourite Saint Paul, the supreme Pioneer, may be roughly styled, following Plato's method through the mouth of the cautious Timaeus, as a fair speculative "likelihood", *the way of the transference of reverence* from static symbols to dynamic realities. In the case before us this way of Rabelaisian thought may be hinted at as follows and the form it takes is a new reconciliation of reason and instinct, a reconciliation according to which both religion and morality, those opposite emotional impulses, are fused and subsumed in a larger and more integral creative energy, an energy which is nothing less than the concentrated action of the individual soul as it deals with the Multiverse of unfathomable dimensions around it.

'I will put the situation as clearly and plainly as I can. Jesus said: "*I* am the way, the truth and the life." Now this saying Saint Paul *transferred to the individual soul* by his profound and original concept of: "Not I, but Christ in me." What Rabelais suggests, according to my "likelihood", is our right to carry this great Pauline advance a step still further and to merge the concept "Christ in us" in the less objective, less symbolic, and much simpler concept of the *deeper soul in us*, that is to say, of the inexhaustible creative energy in the depths of our own individual being. By this bold transference of reverence from the *positive* awe and propitiation and sanctity of Religion, as well as from the *negative* puritanism of Rational Morality, to an unfathomable well-spring of creative force in our own soul, both the unreal systematizations of reason and the too real propitiations of religion are shaken off, and in their place there arises out of the depths the energy that destroys and creates all that exists.'

(*Rabelais*, 1948; IV, ix, 385)

Powys' contention is summed up as follows:

'The "Jesus Christ" who is "the same yesterday, today, and forever" became through the genius of Saint Paul "the Christ in me", that is to say "the Christ in us all".'

(*Rabelais*; IV, ix, 385)

Much, and perhaps all, of that applies to Pope. Powys' 'Christ in us all' blends instinct with Pope's 'God within the mind' (II, 204). Both contend that true virtue is not in danger: Pope's 'God within the mind' acts as a distinguishing faculty, or check, and vice has only to be seen to be hated (II, 218); and Powys quotes Rabelais' statement in the fifty-seventh chapter of *Gargantua* regarding 'an instinct and spur which always drives them on to virtuous deeds and makes them draw back from vice which they call honour'.[1]

It is abundantly clear that such a gospel holds danger: it is as though the only way to the best is just as likely to prove the way to the worst. As Pope neatly puts it, 'our greatest evil' lies disconcertingly close to 'our greatest good' (II, 92). We may clearly agree on the importance of channelling the deeper forces, but surely we want more direction as to *how* this is to be done? That direction Pope does not offer, and this may well appear a weak link, or shaky buttress, in his building; but it is, strangely enough, *at once the poem's central weakness and greatest strength*. For here we can *insert whatever religious beliefs and practices may best suit our particular needs.*[2] The *Essay* has ample room for them. Pope lays, as we have seen, explicit and primary emphasis on 'a mightier Pow'r' than passion (II, 165), and on 'the God within the mind' (II, 204). Such phrases may be supposed to cover much that is usually meant by 'religion'. Here we shall all have different approaches, and for these the *Essay* certainly provides no substitute. It must nevertheless be regarded as not less, but more, comprehensive than any one set of beliefs, roughly corresponding to what we have in mind when we say that the British Empire or Commonwealth finds room for various religions with a creative tolerance suiting the nature of man, the limitations of dogma, and the egotism of personal belief. But such a world-wide system enfolding various religions is itself a super-religion, corresponding to Pope's *Universal Prayer*, and if it be argued that all this is statesmanship and not religion, we can point to our earlier arguments regarding the relative powers of crown and church within the British order (p. 158). Pope himself was never content with anything less than the whole of life, and intended to expand the

[1] IV, ix, 385–6; compare Milton's doctrine of a certain innate 'abstinence' in his *Reason of Church Government*, II, iii; quoted *Christ and Nietzsche*, V, 215, note.

[2] For a discussion of the central importance of the Crucifixion symbol in Christianity with respect to the sublimation of dangerous instincts, see *Christ and Nietzsche*, III, 104–5.

Essay on Man into a greater work involving society, politics, and the nation. His reach is vast, and inclusive. Man's inevitable religious controversies are taken in his stride, and allowed for:

But still this world (so fitted for the knave)
Contents us not. A better shall we have?
A kingdom of the Just then let it be:
But first consider how those Just agree.
The good must merit God's peculiar care;
But who, but God, can tell us who they are?
One thinks on Calvin Heav'n's own spirit fell;
Another deems him instrument of hell;
If Calvin feel Heav'n's blessing, or its rod,
This cries there is, and that, there is no God.
What shocks one part will edify the rest,
Nor with one system can they all be blest.
The very best will variously incline,
And what rewards your Virtue, punish mine.

(IV, 131)

Nevertheless, virtue to Pope remains virtue, whatever the difficulties of assessment. This very indecision, this vacuum at its heart, as it were, is necessary to the *Essay's* whole conception; and in that it commits itself to no dogma, whilst nevertheless presupposing dogma, or some equivalent, at its heart, it corresponds neatly to the British Crown properly understood as a symbol above, and yet containing, all conflicts of party or religion. We, today, expect a world-state, a world-order; and if that new order is to be one of religious tolerance and inclusion, if, as Mr. Custance argues (p. 175), it is to balance correctly the positive and negative, masculine and feminine, principles, in exact descent from Hellenic culture and the New Testament; then we can scarcely do better than take the *Essay on Man* as our guide. Here we draw close to a new understanding of Byron's powerful intuition of Pope as 'the national poet of mankind' (p. 160).

Pope has, however, left us certain pregnant religious assertions of his own. His seraphs and angels are impregnated with a burning conviction that somehow stops short of any dogmatic limitation; you feel that if you don't like those terms, you can call them something else, but you do not question their reality. As for the lovely passage starting 'Submit—in this or any other sphere' (I, 285–94;

quoted p. 46), it is surely as good a practical definition of faith as any you will discover, expanding the New Testament assertion that the hairs of our heads are all numbered and that no sparrow falls to the ground without God's knowledge. Pope's lines, perhaps especially his exquisite equating of 'chance' with 'direction', give lucid and memorable expression to a *living* truth, existing in the order not of thought, but of life. The more you live with them, the truer they become; the more you accept the harmony, the more of it you find, and create, around you. They are creatively, dynamically, true.

Such is the basis of Pope's *Essay*, and here is, as surely, its heart:

So Man, who here seems principal alone,
Perhaps acts second to some sphere unknown,
Touches some wheel, or verges to some goal;
'Tis but a part we see, and not a whole.

(I, 57)

That 'sphere' or 'wheel' symbolizes those higher dimensions elsewhere in poetry expressed by temples, domes, urns, circles of various sorts; and without some such intuition, we shall drop to the level of those whose clouded thinking cannot conceive that the supernatural machinery of those spirits of the dead (I, 47–66) called 'sylphs', which Pope added to the first version of *The Rape of the Lock* and regarded as the greatest proof of judgement he had ever shown,[1] may indeed correspond to what actually goes on around us as surely as the card game and coffee-pots of that richly devised poem. Nor must we forget that other guardian spirit, the sainted maid of *Eloisa to Abelard*. Pope's poetic meaning will never be received without fullest honours accorded to the sovereignty of such intuitions. Through them he labours to integrate human existence within the higher dimensions, as a space-time concern blending impulse with value in tune with the eternal: he is trying to see life as art.

The two driving forces in Pope's work are: (i) his devotion to poetry, and (ii) his passion for a genuine ethic. These are twin aspects of a single ideal. If, in reading his early *Essay on Criticism*, you make, as I have made in lectures now for twenty years, point by point transferences to the art of life, you get some interesting results that may serve to supplement and interpret the *Essay on Man*; and the complexities of the later essay force us continually to speak in terms of drama. In both art and ethic Pope stresses the need for vitality:

[1] Spence, 142; quoted Tillotson, 'Design', 56.

his *Inferno*, *The Dunciad*, is full of dull writers; but he is not thinking of entertainment.

Vitality conditions penetration, insight and virtue. The business of poetry is involved closely with what we mean by 'eternity', and so is the business of man. In the great campaign of peace, when the old problems are gone, man must advance. He is, and will remain, dynamic, for good or for ill. The *Essay on Man* prepares for this, without fully succeeding in illustration of what must follow; for, after most admirably defining man's task of integration, it leaves us, in the later sections, with little more than a fine counsel of vital contentment and goodness, together, it must be admitted, with some slackening of poetic vigour. There are exquisite passages, there is wisdom and brilliance, but some of the sap has gone. Now this is just where Nietzsche so strongly diverges. We have talked much of 'sublimation', but, were the positive powers in man truly captured and released, and no one is more anxious for a full incorporation of all our most *secret* impulses than Pope, something very strange might come of it. The sublimation that merely results in morality as normally understood may be, at least where genius is concerned, a specious sublimation, veiling poisons, and that is what all our denunciatory satirists are trying to say, from the New Testament onwards. What they are driving at is, whether they know it or not, a consummation greater, and rather frightening. Pope himself knew that he struck fear into his contemporaries.[1] Exactly what the new virtue, or greatness, is to be, we cannot say, except that it will hold traffic with higher dimensions of existence. Now, though Pope insists strongly on the reality of the superhuman powers, he strikes out no such ambitious programme for man himself. He insists that humanity should keep its station. But that very concentration on man which he counsels, involving, as it does, a realization of his physical and mental limitations, becomes, by forcing an acceptance of man's passions and their 'mysterious use' (*Essays on Man*, II, 206), a valuable advance; that very intellectual humility on which he insists itself throws open the way to an infinitude of super-rational possibilities. Pope's emphasis on man as man's proper study is at once humility and pride since, though the honest facing of instinct demands humility, the natural results of that honesty may, with God's help, be expected to flower in self-transcendence. His counsel of contentment with man's lot on earth may accordingly be said to feed that inmost Promethean spark

[1] IV, 266; also *Satires, Epilogue*, II, 209; see pp. 55, 76.

which cannot remain content. Pope has sown the seed; the rest has been, and is being, carried on by others. Here we touch the paradox of his personal studies, Sir Plume, Atossa, Sporus, presented statically, yet each a dynamo; poetically still, yet swirling with energies; creatures of art, of space-time.

And what Pope's explicit thinking does not formulate, his symbolisms and phraseology continually suggest:

> *Th' Eternal Art educing good from ill,*
> *Grafts on this Passion our best principle:*
> *'Tis thus the Mercury of Man is fix'd,*
> *Strong grows the Virtue with his nature mix'd.*
>
> (II, 175)

There is a great adventure, maybe a great experiment, afoot, far beyond our comprehension; there is an injunction on man to *make* something of himself, though what exactly we cannot easily say. The New Testament is our guide, and *Thus Spake Zarathustra*, pointing to a righteousness beyond the righteousness of Scribe and Pharisee, and to a life of balance, poise and power. The exact destination, whether on this plane or another, we shall not visualize: we only know that we are invited to collaborate with the Eternal Artist.

POSTSCRIPT

THOSE to whom the lines of approach suggested throughout this book appear interesting would do well to read two valuable contributions on 'eternity' and the modern mind: *A Crisis in Human Affairs*, by J. G. Bennett (1948), and *Release from Time*, by C. Conway Plumbe (1950).

It is, I think, significant that the space-time and sense-blending qualities of poetic symbolism discussed on pp. 80–91 above correspond closely to reports received by trance-communication purporting to come from higher planes: a good recent example is A. Borgia's *Life in the World Unseen* (1954).

Relevant thoughts occur also in Joanna Field's *A Life of One's Own* (1934; *Pelican Books*, 1952), and Aldous Huxley's *The Doors of Perception* (1954). To these I might add that religious classic of the last century, Henry Drummond's *Natural Law in the Spiritual World.*

The time has surely passed when great poetry can be profitably discussed without attention to such advances.

INDEX

Fictional persons, quotations, etc., are indexed under the works to which they belong.

References applying to foot-notes are given page numerals only.